NEW TESTAMENT
EVERYDAY BIBLE STUDIES

HEBREWS

LIVING A LONG FAITHFULNESS

SCOT MCKNIGHT

QUESTIONS WRITTEN BY
BECKY CASTLE MILLER

Harper*Christian*
Resources

New Testament Everyday Bible Study Series: Hebrews
© 2025 by Scot McKnight

Published by HarperChristian Resources, 3950 Sparks Drive SE, Suite 101, Grand Rapids, MI 49546, USA. HarperChristian Resources is a registered trademark of HarperCollins Christian Publishing, Inc.

Requests for information should be sent to customercare@harpercollins.com.

ISBN 978-0-310-12953-0 (softcover)
ISBN 978-0-310-12954-7 (ebook)

HarperChristian Resources titles may be purchased in bulk for church, business, fundraising, or ministry use. For information, please e-mail ResourceSpecialist@ChurchSource.com.

First Printing August 2025 / Printed in the United States of America
25 26 27 28 29 LBC 5 4 3 2 1

CONTENTS

For Lucy and Nick

GENERAL INTRODUCTION

Christians make a claim for the Bible not made of any other book. Or, since the Bible is a library shelf of many authors, it's a claim we make of no other shelf of books. We claim that God worked in each of the authors as they were writing so that what was scratched on papyrus expressed what God wanted communicated to the people of God. Which makes the New Testament (NT) a book unlike any other book. Which is why Christians are reading the NT almost two thousand years later with great delight. These books have the power to instruct us and to rebuke us and to correct us and to train us to walk with God every day. We read these books because God speaks to us in them.

Developing a routine of reading the Bible with an open heart, a receptive mind, and a flexible will is the why of the *New Testament Everyday Bible Studies*. But not every day will be the same. Some days we pause and take it in and other days we stop and repent and lament and open ourselves to God's restoring graces. No one word suffices for what the Bible does to us. In fact, the Bible's view of the Bible can be found by reading Psalm 119, the longest chapter in the Bible with 176 verses! It is a meditation on eight terms for what the Bible is and what the Bible does to those who listen and read it. Its laws instruct us and order us, its statutes direct us, its precepts inform us, its decrees guide us, its commands compel us, its words speak to us, and its promises comfort us, and it is no wonder that the author can sum all eight up as the "way" (119:3). Each of those terms still speaks to what happens when we open our minds to the Word of God.

Every day with the Bible then is new because our timeless and timely God communes with us in our daily lives in our world and in our time, just as God spoke to Jesus in Galilee and Paul in Ephesus and John on Patmos. These various contexts help us hear God in our context, so the New Testament Everyday Bible Studies will often delve into contexts. Most of us now have a Bible on our devices. We may well have several translations available to us everywhere we go, every day. To hear those words, we are summoned by God to open the Bible, to attune our hearts to God, and to listen to what he says. My prayer is that these daily study guides will help each of us become daily Bible readers attentive to the mind of God. Even our prayers, which may well evoke something for which we are responsible, are sustained by the prayers of the Lord for us, and as our text informs us, he is always praying for us (Hebrews 7:25).

INTRODUCTION: READING THE BOOK OF HEBREWS

By the time the author of Hebrews pushed send, a very serious issue was disturbing the churches under his care. Faithfulness was the challenge. Could these believers live a long faithfulness? Not a faithfulness in spurts one year and then nothing the next. Not a faithfulness that was electrified by a big action but lacked daily allegiance. What they needed was to follow Jesus faithfully, every day, all day long, every week, every month, and every year for the rest of their lives. I am calling this a long faithfulness. It's not easy, even if you try. To complicate the explicit challenges, the author of Hebrews frequently uses the term *perfection* for long faithfulness. Since perfection stretches well beyond the attainable and smacks of sinlessness if not unhealthy scrupulosity, it may be helpful for all of us if we understand perfection in Hebrews as *long faithfulness*.

Long in long faithfulness does not need to mean legalism or sinlessness. We can approach this important theme in the book of Hebrews from a different beginning (other than with ourselves and our obedience). God's faithfulness, which is longer than long, empowers our long faithfulness, and our faithfulness is but a moment in God's. God's long faithfulness sustains our faithfulness. The book of Hebrews declares for each of us that "he who promised is faithful" (10:23; cf. 11:11). The faithful Promiser is a faithful Empowerer. Reading this one-of-a-kind document requires that we begin with God and his Son, as Hebrews does (1:1), and not with our struggle to maintain a long faithfulness. God's long faithfulness shapes our calling to be faithful on every page of this letter. We can too easily get trapped in wondering if our faithfulness is long enough, when the truth is that God's faithfulness is what is longer beyond length, and higher beyond height, and deeper beyond depth. Because God's vast faithfulness empowers our faithfulness. Yet, we are responsible to enter into God's long faithfulness, not by stretching ourselves out, but by trusting, worshiping, and embracing God's unlimited length, height, and depth.

The long faithfulness in the book of Hebrews points to God's will and doing it, and God's will in the pages of Scripture means loving God and loving others. It means pursuing justice and peace and wisdom, it means living in the Spirit, and it means following the teachings of Jesus. Long faithfulness cannot be reduced to what many would call *spirituality*, nor can it be reduced to one's personal interactive relationship with God, with all its highs and lows. Yes, that relationship roots us in God, but long faithfulness reflects a life that is inner and outer, personal and social, and exercised in communion with other people of faith.

In the book of Hebrews life is a journey, a pilgrimage, a walking on a singular path behind Jesus, the Pioneer and Perfecter of our long faithfulness. The aim of long faithfulness is the Rest, which otherwise can be called the kingdom of God, the heavenly city, or eternal salvation. In the Rest, the believers will experience the fullness of perfection, purification, forgiveness, holiness, transformation, and salvation. Believers always face sin; they need the resolution of sin through Jesus Christ's life, death, burial, resurrection, ascension, and session (or sitting) at the right hand of the Father as the one who now intercedes for us. The believer faces sin daily as they seek to follow Jesus in the journey from wherever they are to their final Rest in the presence of God.

The theological themes of Hebrews complicate themselves because they form into a network of first century sensibilities. Many of those sensibilities are not known to us today. Eugene Peterson expressed how many think of Hebrews when he wrote that it "is a tangle of argument and obscurity" (Peterson, *Lights a Lovely Mile,* 107). Part of the ambiguity forms into wonderments about the audience. What we can infer confidently is that Hebrews addresses some Christians with a squishy commitment to following Jesus. Frankly, we don't know much about that audience, even though confidence shines brightly for some who write or preach about it. What we know is that they needed to be exhorted and warned, and we know they were facing suffering and social abuse from non-believers. We don't know if they were Jewish or gentile.

The author roots his strong exhortations in comparisons of the Son to angels, to Moses, to Melchizedek, and to the entire tabernacle/temple system: the covenant, the high priest, and the sacrifices. Because Jesus fulfills each of them, Jesus is better than each. Because of who he is and what he has accomplished, the summons to long faithfulness becomes doable. Interspersing these intense comparisons are exhortations to a long faithfulness. To help readers understand the theological themes in Hebrews, I created an Appendix that cuts out the warning passages. One can read that Appendix front to back and experience more directly how theologically shaped this book is.

A recent trend among those who study Hebrews is worth mentioning here. We are accustomed to saying Jesus' death is atoning—that at the cross our sins were forgiven. Yet, this book pokes that belief in the eye because it neglects the resurrection and, even more, the ascension and session. Today more and more believe our atonement transcends Good Friday and Easter Sunday to include the event that happened forty days later, at the ascension and the session. I acknowledge my own neglect of ascension, and in this Everyday Bible Study I will take steps toward affirming ascension as integral to our own redemption. Not until Jesus sat down was his work of redemption complete (and perfected).

I've worked hard to keep the words *letter* and *epistle* from being mentioned above. Hebrews is not really a letter. It doesn't open like one, it doesn't sound like one throughout, and its ending informs us what is written is a "word of exhortation" (13:22). But immediately before and after that, it echoes words from other letters (13:19, 23–24). So, it has been called a letter, as well as its more official term, *epistle*. I've read hundreds of ancient letters, and I've not seen one like Hebrews. So, I prefer a different genre classification.

Most today think Hebrews is a sermon, but since (1) *sermon* sounds like something we hear for twenty to forty-five minutes on Sunday morning, and (2) this book doesn't sound like anything any of us hears on a Sunday morning, and (3) if it did, it would be way too long for our Sunday services, I suggest we will need to modify what we think a sermon is to fit what *this* Sermon is! Most today recognize that this Sermon echoes sermons given in synagogues. The sermon Paul delivered in Pisidian Antioch (Acts 13:14–15) uses the very expression (*word of exhortation*) that Hebrews uses for itself (Hebrews 13:22). So, think of Hebrews as a formal sermonic lecture, instruction, or address. If one wanted to go one step higher in culture, it could be called an *oration*. There is no shooting from the hip, nothing casual or flippant or feel-good, not a hint of megachurch preachers wearing blue jeans with long-tailed shirts untucked. There is nothing in the entire Sermon ill-prepared. If this was a sermon, it was written up and read out loud. Only by ending like a letter does the Sermon take on the feel of a letter.

Alongside this genre issue is the authorship question. Hebrews was not written by the Apostle Paul, even if in the history of the church many claimed it was. The Greek of this letter is unlike anything—very much unlike, in fact—attached to Paul's name. Students who have learned to read the Greek of Paul are unable to make sense of the Greek of Hebrews, and that has always revealed much to me. In fact, Paul denounces the use of the kind of rhetoric we find in Hebrews (cf. 1 Corinthians 2:1–5; 2 Corinthians 11:5). To take but one example of a difference: Paul quotes the Old Testament because Scripture has authority. In this Sermon the preacher cites God, the Son, and the Spirit quoting Scriptures (see Peeler, *Hebrews*, 17). Furthermore, Paul would not say he heard the gospel from witnesses because he claimed over and over that he encountered Jesus himself (cf. Galatians 1:11–17 to Hebrews 2:2–4).

One suggestion of who wrote Hebrews is as good as any other. Even the smidgeons of evidence some claim we have doesn't amount to enough to attach this wonderful book to a name. Let's just agree it was a man or woman in the churches of the city of Rome who had some connection to the Apostle Paul and be done with it. Someone like Aquila and/or Priscilla, but that's not a claim to their or her or his authorship. Amy Peeler offers wisdom when she says it was "written by a member of the broad Pauline network of gospel ministers" (Peeler, *Hebrews*, 18). Whoever wrote this amazing Sermon knew the Old Testament deeply, had a wonderful facility in Greek, and could draft up an intensive sermon into an extensive exhortation with considerable rhetorical skill. A list of possible names would include Luke, Clement,

Barnabas, Silas, Apollos, and Priscilla. We don't know for sure, and we should just admit that. In this Bible study, I will call the author "Instructor."

The Instructor of this book, unlike the apostle Paul, has no personality, or at least no personality throbs in this text and pokes itself out for all of us to hear and imagine. Listen to the frank admission of Amy Peeler:

> I have often puzzled over my lack of "connection" to this author. Having closely studied this sermon for over a decade, I feel little sense of camaraderie with the person who wrote it. That could be an individual deficiency on my part, but in comparison with the letters of Paul, on which I have not spent as much time, the difference is striking. I feel that I know Paul and cannot wait to have particular discussions with him in the Kingdom of God. Conversely, the author of Hebrews remains largely a blank slate, an unknowable mystery. Instead of frustration with this person's demureness, I am impressed with the way in which he has so thoroughly drawn his listeners' attention to God. I may feel little to no connection with whoever this may be, but I do love—deeply—what this author has written. (Peeler, *Hebrews*, 20)

The author's lack of personal revelation in this Sermon fits with the title I give him: Instructor. The title may not be warm, but it throws our attention onto his text, which is precisely what he wants to happen. *Mark these words*, he is saying, *not who wrote them*.

The audience of the Sermon has been assigned by title to "the Hebrews," which is either polished or condescending for "Jews" or "Judeans" (the English term *Jew* derives from "Judah" and "Judea," and thus the term echoes a geographical location). We will turn to the famous words of Hebrews 6 when we get there, but at this point I want to say that there is no clear evidence the audience was returning to Judaism. The problem was persecution, defection, and apostasy. The audience was challenged to choose the Lord Jesus instead of the ways of the world and the gods of this age. On the date of this Sermon, since the temple is not mentioned as having been destroyed, it could have been written and sent pre–73 AD (Peeler, Pierce). On the location, the brief note "from Italy" in 13:24, could mean the Instructor was in Italy (Rome), or it could have been written from somewhere else to Italy when the author was with some believers from Italy. Or, the letter could have been sent from Italy to Jerusalem, Galilee, or Alexandria, and he was with some from Italy. Most today think the Sermon was sent to Rome, and I can live with that as long as we don't get too confident about it.

In reading this Sermon straight through, you will feel the interruptions of the Warning passages. They are found at 2:1–4, 3:7–4:13, 5:11–6:12, 10:19–39, and also at 12:4–29. If you skip them in reading the letter, you will find a rather orderly set of comparisons between Jesus and the covenant system found in the Old Testament (Appendix). The letter begins with an astounding statement about the Son (1:1–4), who becomes the central theme of the entire Sermon by way of the following eight comparisons. These comparisons become noteworthy in their use of the term *better* (see sidebar: "'Better' Things in Hebrews," pp. 105–107).

1. The Son and Angels (1:5–14; 2:5–18)
2. The Son and Moses (3:1–6)
3. The Son and the High Priest (4:14–5:10)
4. The Son and Melchizedek (6:13–7:28)
5. The Son and the Covenant (8:1–13)
6. The Son and the Tabernacle (9:1–28)

7. The Son and Sacrifice (10:1–18)
8. The Son and Faith (11:1–12:3)

These comparisons are then followed by a chapter about long faithfulness's kind of faith (11:1–12:3), with a long warning (12:4–29), and then the ending to the letter (13:1–25).

FOR FURTHER READING

Eugene H. Peterson, *Lights a Lovely Mile: Collected Sermons of the Church Year* (Colorado Springs: WaterBrook, 2023).

WORKS CITED IN THE STUDY GUIDE

(Throughout this guide you will find the author's name and title in brackets, as noted in this book listing, with page numbers whenever I cite something from it):

Gareth Lee Cockerill, *Yesterday, Today, and Forever: Listening to Hebrews in the Twenty-First Century* (Eugene, Oregon: Cascade, 2022). [Cockerill, *Hebrews*]
David A. deSilva, *Hebrews: Grace and Gratitude* (Nashville: Abingdon, 2020). [DeSilva, *Hebrews*]
James Earl Massey, updated by Jennifer T. Kaalund, "Hebrews," in Brian K. Blount, Gay L. Byron, Emerson B. Powery, *True to Our Native Land: An African American New Testament Commentary*, 2nd edition (Minneapolis: Fortress, 2024), 471–487. [Massey-Kaalund, "Hebrews"]

Scot McKnight, *The Second Testament: A New Translation* (Downers Grove: IVP Academic, 2023. [*Second Testament*]

On the warning passages, I make use of my article "The Warning Passages of Hebrews: A Formal Analysis and Theological Conclusions," *Trinity Journal* 13 (1992): 21–59.

Amy Peeler, *Hebrews* (Commentaries for Christian Formation; Grand Rapids: Wm. B. Eerdmans, 2024). [Peeler, *Hebrews*]

Madison Pierce, "Letter to the Hebrews," in eds. Esau McCaulley, Janette H. Ok, Osvaldo Padilla, Amy Peeler, *The New Testament in Color: A Multiethnic Bible Commentary* (Downers Grove: IVP Academic, 2024), 581–609. [Pierce, "Hebrews"]

THE FAITHFUL GOD
AND THE SON-WORD

Hebrews 1:1–4

(reformatted)

[1] In the past
God spoke
to our ancestors
through the prophets
at many times and in various ways,
[2] but in these last days he has spoken to us by his Son,
whom he appointed heir of all things,
and through whom also he made the universe.
[3] The Son is the radiance of God's glory
and the exact representation of his being,
sustaining all things by his powerful word.
After he had provided purification for sins,
he sat down at the right hand of the Majesty in heaven.
[4] So he became as much superior to the angels
as the name he has inherited is superior to theirs.

God has always communicated with humans. But God only fully communicated with humans in the face of God's Son. We can call the Son here the "Son-Word of God." In Jesus Christ we see the fullness of who God is, what God does, and what God wills for all creation. As the Son-Word of God, Jesus is unlike anything else that reveals God and unlike any other human. As the Son-Word of God, Jesus is better than various features in the story and practices of Israel.

Lines as aesthetically designed as these are deserving more than an ordinary paragraph of prose. Unfortunately, most translations do just that. To echo the aesthetical beauty of these opening verses to the Sermon, I reformatted the NIV in a way similar to my own translation (McKnight, *Second Testament*). In Greek, the entirety of verse one is the *subject* of the verb in verse two! That is, "The God who spoke [back then, in all those ways] spoke to us in these last days." One more feature of this beautiful introduction: The following words all begin with the Greek letter *pi* (*p*, π): "past" and "ancestors" and "prophets" and "many times" and "various ways." David deSilva reproduces those *p*'s in his translation: "piece meal and partial were God's past pronouncements to the patriarchs through the prophets" (deSilva, *Hebrews*, 19).

GOD SPOKE

Though the NIV starts with "In the past God," the original text begins with "in many places and in many patterns." This will set up the time of God's multivariant speaking to humans, which was "in the past" (1:1). The Instructor does not care about what God communicated in creation or in the heart of humans. His concern is God's multivariant speech "through the prophets." That is, the prophets in the Instructor's Bible, roughly equivalent to our Old Testament. Robert Alter's magnificent translation of the Hebrew Bible is in three volumes: the law of Moses, the prophets, and the writings. The Instructor has Alter's second volume in mind. Yet, because the Instructor cites texts from throughout all three of those sections in the Old Testament, we are wise to think he saw the entire Scriptures as written by prophets.

Only in grasping God's speaking through God's prophets can one grasp either God's communication to humans or God's communication in the Son. The revelation of God in the Son fulfills, expands, and extends what God had said in the past through the prophets. Yet, what God speaks in the Son is entirely consistent with what God has said in the past. The Old Testament, then, is not some relic, nor is it of interest for nostalgia. Rather, it is God's communication that alone makes sense of the Son-Word of God. The New Testament is to the Old Testament what a computer is to a typewriter—the same and altogether new all at the same time. (Just ask those of us older than sixty.) As Amy Peeler has written, "This filial speech, speech in a person who is God's begotten, is not a response to a failure of communication in the prophetic mode but the goal for which all the other communication was preparing" (Peeler, *Hebrews*, 41). If we diminish the Old Testament, we degrade God, the Son, and the Spirit. If we diminish the Old Testament, we degrade the New Testament.

THE SON-WORD OF GOD

That complex communication from God to God's people through prophets came to its fulfillment in Jesus Christ, the Son-Word of God (1:2–4). If we let them, these verses will probe us to ask ourselves what we think of Jesus. In particular, we will ask if we think of Jesus in as exalted of terms as the Instructor lays out in the lines of today's reading. The exalted Son-Word of God remains faithful to us, and with such an exalted person at our side we can live a long faithfulness.

Let this then be said: The Instructor opens by magnifying Jesus Christ as God's Son, the very Word spoken by God. He doesn't begin this Sermon by talking about himself; he doesn't emote his feelings for his audience; and he doesn't outline what he's about to say. He brags about Jesus. Nothing else, nothing less, nothing more. If we follow the Instructor's strategy, we will always begin with Jesus. The Word of God has a face, and it's the face of Jesus. We need to wonder what God is saying to us, and we don't need to wander into our own thoughts and discernments about what God is saying. God has spoken, and the Word spoken is "Jesus." As Eugene Peterson once preached, "Mary's firstborn is God's last word," and that what Israel's long and longer story "needed was not another commentary but a conclusion—not another book but a last chapter to the book they already had" (Peterson, *Lights a Lovely Mile*, 23, 26). This opening paragraph to the Sermon ought to prompt each of us to spend more time with Jesus by reading the Gospels as well as the Old Testament Jesus himself knew.

Much is said about the Son in these three words, beginning with (a) Jesus being God's communication "in these last days" (1:2). This doesn't mean the end of time. Rather, it means the last message God has for God's people in this world. In Jesus the last days begin, and the next moment in God's plan is the kingdom of God's full arrival. God not only speaks the Son-Word but God "appointed" Jesus to be (b) "heir of all things," which will be on full display when the final kingdom arrives. From the final future to the beginning of beginnings, the Instructor then says of Jesus that God "made the universe" (c) through him. But the translation "universe" suggests the materiality of creation when the term itself suggests time itself. The Instructor chose a term better translated as "Eras," or what is often translated as "ages." The Instructor wants us to keep our minds fixed on the plan of

God in history, the unfolding of time and God's redemptive plan, and he wants us to know that Jesus is both the origin and the goal of all time!

The Wisdom of God in the Wisdom of Solomon and Hebrews 1:3

The following text is found in the Old Testament's apocryphal text called "The Wisdom of Solomon," and what is said here of wisdom shows parallels with what the Instructor says about Jesus.

For she is a breath of the power of God
and a pure emanation of the glory of the Almighty;
therefore nothing defiled gains entrance into her.

For she is a *reflection* [same as radiance in
        Hebrews] of eternal light,
a spotless mirror of the working of God,
and an image of his goodness.

Although she is but one, she can do all things,
and while remaining in herself, she renews all things;
in every generation she passes into holy souls
and makes them friends of God and prophets,

for God loves nothing so much as the person
        who lives with wisdom.
She is more beautiful than the sun
and excels every constellation of the stars.
Compared with the light she is found to be more
        radiant,

> for it is succeeded by the night,
> but against wisdom evil does not prevail.
> She reaches mightily from one end of the earth to
>   the other,
>
> and she orders all things well. (Wisdom of
>   Solomon 7:25–8:1, NRSVue)

From these three observations about Jesus, the Instructor moves to terms about who Jesus is in this Son-Word of God (1:3). He is (d) the "radiance of God's glory" and (e) "the exact representation of his being" (1:3). Radiance can be active in the sense that the Son radiates the glory of God (cf. 2 Peter 1:19). But it could also be passive in the sense that the Son reflects the glory of God. Since the second term ("representation") evokes the passive sense, it is more likely that Jesus here actively radiates the glories of who he is, somewhat the way lava in a volcano radiates the heat and colors of what lies below the surface of a volcano. As the one who represents, Jesus is a precise and perfect depiction of the very "being" of God. What makes God God is who Jesus is. He is like a stamp's impression on wax, with God as the stamp and Jesus as the impression.

The Instructor cannot say enough, so he moves on: The Son-Word of God (f) is "sustaining all things by his powerful world" (1:3). The Son is not only the creator and the goal, but the Son radiates and depicts who God is throughout history, and in the middle of that history, in these last days, the Son has "provided purification for sins," accomplishing what the law required (1:3). In "purification" we meet a term (cf. 9:13, 14, 22, 23; 10:2, 22) that will be but one term among many about purity, the temple, sacrifice, priests, and the redemption the Son provides. Purity describes a condition (a person) or a setting (the temple) or a thing (an altar) or an animal (a lamb) fit for the presence of God. To purify, then, is to clear the way for God's presence. Jesus purifies to make us fit for God's presence, which is the final end to our journey of long faithfulness.

In these last days the Son not only revealed God and accomplished redemption but then capped it off when he "sat down at the right hand of the Majesty in heaven" (1:3). Once again, the time element mentioned above comes to the fore. The Instructor provides for his audience a sketch of the major moments in the life of the Son-Word of God. As I mentioned in the introduction, the redemptive work of the Son cannot be reduced to his life, to his death, or to his resurrection. His work is finished only when he takes the seat next to the Father.

Because of who he is and what he has accomplished, in sitting at the right hand of the Majesty, the Son "became as much superior," or "so much better" (*Second Testament*) than "the angels as the name he has inherited" "carries so much more weight than theirs" (1:4, *Second Testament*). No other creation sits at the right hand of God, and no other creation can be called "Son" by the Father. The word *Son* is found twenty-one times in Hebrews. Notice especially 1:5, 8; 3:6; 4:14; 5:5, 8; 7:3, 28. Jesus alone is the Son of the one and only Father.

QUESTIONS FOR REFLECTION AND APPLICATION

1. As you begin this study, what are your first impressions of the idea of living a long faithfulness as a Christian?

2. How did the prophets function as conduits of God's speech to God's people in the past?

3. How does the Son communicate God's words to God's people?

4. What does it mean for Jesus to be the radiance and representation of God?

5. In what ways do you need the purifying work of Jesus in your life as you seek to live out long faithfulness?

FOR FURTHER READING

Eugene Peterson, *Lights a Lovely Mile: Collected Sermons of the Church Year* (Colorado Springs: WaterBrook, 2023).

GOD TALKS ABOUT THE SON AND THE ANGELS

Hebrews 1:5–14

(emphasis added)

[5] *For to which of the angels did* **God** *ever say,*

> *"You are my Son;*
>> *today I have become your Father"? [Psalm 2:7]*

Or again [God says],

> *"I will be his Father,*
>> *and he will be my Son"? [2 Samuel 7:14 or*
>> *1 Chronicles 17:13]*

[6] *And again, when God brings his firstborn into the world,* **he [God]** *says,*

> *"Let all God's angels worship him."*
>> *[Deuteronomy 32:43]*

⁷ In speaking of the angels **he [God]** says,

> "He makes his angels spirits,
>> and his servants flames of fire." [Psalm 104:4]

⁸ But about the Son **he [God]** says,

> "Your throne, O God, will last for ever and ever;
>> a scepter of justice will be the scepter of your kingdom.
> ⁹ You have loved righteousness and hated wickedness;
>> therefore God, your God, has set you above your
>>> companions
>> by anointing you with the oil of joy." [Psalm 45:5–6]

¹⁰ **He [God]** also says [the Greek has only "and" here],

> "In the beginning, Lord, you laid the foundations of
>> the earth,
>> and the heavens are the work of your hands.
> ¹¹ They will perish, but you remain;
>> they will all wear out like a garment.
> ¹² You will roll them up like a robe;
>> like a garment they will be changed.
> But you remain the same,
>> and your years will never end." [Psalm 102:25–27]

¹³ To which of the angels did **God** ever say,

> "[You] Sit at my right hand
>> until I make your enemies
>> a footstool for your feet"? [Psalm 110:1]

¹⁴ Are not all angels ministering spirits sent to serve those who
will inherit salvation?

On the table next to my desk I have five translations of the Bible. Actually, two of those are only of the Old Testament. On my desk I have a Greek New Testament, an NIV Bible, and *The Second Testament*, all open to Hebrews 1. On the monitor I have Accordance, a piece of Bible software, which is open to Hebrews 1 in both the NIV and the Greek. With a click on Accordance I can access dozens of Bibles and tools to study the Bible. As someone sitting in the aisles with the older folks, I can be quite amazed at what I have available to me now when I study the Bible.

If I want to know where "angel" is used in the Bible, I can type the word *angel* and search an English translation. I just searched, and in the NIV the word *angel* appears 195 times. To nuance that search, I looked up one of the Hebrew terms for *angel (mlk)*, and it occurs, because it doesn't always mean *angel*, 196 times. The Greek word for *angel (angelos)* occurs 171 times in the New Testament, and it, too, does not always mean *angel*. In case you're wondering how someone can add 196 plus 171 and get 195, one can't. The uses of the Hebrew and Greek terms don't always refer to an angelic being. So, let's give the NIV translators the benefit of the doubt and say there are about 200 instances of a word referring to an angel in the Bible. It's easy, even if it takes time, to go through each instance. *Whether we know a thing about the Bible or not, we can find each instance with a click.* With software attached to our digital Bibles, we can get commentary, background, and devotional reflections.

They Knew the Bible Well

If you keep two ribbon bookmarks plus all five fingers of one hand in the Old Testament passages being cited by the Instructor and the other hand opened to today's reading, you will be given a lesson on how the earliest Christians read the Old Testament. Most of us have learned to read the Bible *devotionally*—that is, we read it to hear God speak to us personally. Fewer have learned to read the Bible grammatically—that is, by diagramming sentences. Some have learned to read the Bible in its historical context, but that takes a lot of work, finding and reading ancient sources. Some have learned to read the Bible by author, and they can distinguish Paul from Hebrews from John. Others have learned to read the Bible theologically and can put together passages from hither and yon in the Bible and score points about what the Bible says about X or Y or Z topic.

Now take a deep breath: *None of us reads the Bible the way Jesus and the first century Christians read the Bible.* Those early Christians did not own a copy of the Bible; all they knew about the Bible was either in their memory or what they heard from a teacher or a scribe or a rabbi.

What you find in today's reading displays how well the Instructor knew the Bible. His specialty seems to have been psalms about David, often called the *royal psalms*. He cites from Psalm 2, then probably 2 Samuel 7 (or perhaps the parallel at 1 Chronicles 17), then from Deuteronomy 32 (and here it looks like he knows the alternative reading of that passage that shows up in the Dead Sea Scrolls),* and then back to Psalm 104, followed by two longer quotations from the Psalms (45, 102), and closes with a short citation from the most commonly cited passage in the New Testament, Psalm 110. Most of us can't do this. What we can learn from the Instructor is that, if we want to know the fullness of what God has said to us in the Son-Word of God, we will need to become Bible readers. People become Bible readers

---

* In brief, "Let all God's angels worship him" is not found in the traditional Hebrew text but is found in the Septuagint and in the Dead Sea Scrolls, so the most recent translations now include this line (e.g., the NIV).

by reading the Bible over and over. An old man in the church in which I grew up used to say at times that he had read the Bible through once a year for more than fifty years (and he may have said sixty). A saintly old man, he could quote Bible verses as well as the Instructor.

THE BIBLE IS GOD TALKING

I confess that I'm trained to think historically about the Bible; that is, when I am writing academic books. My approach is to ask *who* the author was, *when* the author wrote this book, *what* the context was for that author writing that book, and other questions, like *how* this book or this verse relates to similar ideas in the ancient world. So, when I read Isaiah, I'm asking what Isaiah meant. Please notice *who the Instructor names as the speaker or writer* of these varied texts from the Old Testament. I have put this author in bold font. The author, for him, of each of the citations was God (Hebrews 1:5, 6, 7, 8, 10, 13). God talks to and about his Son in today's passage. You might need to pause to take that in.

My approach, which focuses on the author in historical context, is not wrong. But the Instructor might say to me, *Please take the next step, Scot, and ask what God is saying in this text.* Which is how I have approached writing these Everyday Bible Study guides. We get to look through the author's words into the words of God. In his recent academic study, Kevin Vanhoozer, a theologian, describes the Instructor's approach to Bible reading like this: "God is the primary cause of our understanding, then, and illumination is shorthand for the Spirit's work of interpretive grace whereby he grants us what we need to understand what we are reading: the eyes to discern the light of Christ . . . in the letter of the text" (Vanhoozer, *Mere Christian Hermeneutics*, 345).

The Instructor, then, encourages us to hear the voice of God when we read the Scriptures. This does not mean we leave our heads in the other room when we read the Bible. We do not attribute to God, say, the words of Satan in Job or the temptation narrative of Jesus. What the Instructor wants us to know is that the Bible speaks the Word of God to us, and that in reading and listening to the Bible, we can hear God speak.

What the Instructor also wants us to know is that the Father speaks to the Son. This entire passage is a "conversation . . . primarily between the Father and the Son" (Pierce, "Hebrews," 584). You can see this if you fasten upon God/ Father using second personal singulars (e.g., you; 1:5, 8, 9, 10, 11, 12) and the You is implied at 1:13's "[You] Sit . . ." The Father speaks also to the angels (1:7; *Second Testament*; the NIV has "in speaking *of* the angels"). Amy Peeler, recognizing the Greek's sense of toward, suggests "and gesturing toward the angels, God says" (Peeler, *Hebrews*, 59).

THEY SAW JESUS AS GOD

Perhaps the most important element for Bible reading that I see in Hebrews 1 is that the Instructor sees Jesus in places many might not have seen him, and the Jesus he sees is fully God. As God, he is God's Son, which was early Christian language for Jesus as God's royal Son (cf. Mark 1:11; 9:7; Romans 1:1–5). (Notice the underlined words in the text in today's Scripture reading.) The text of Psalm 2 is about David, but since David anticipates the Messiah, and Jesus is the Messiah, the Instructor sees Jesus in "You are my son, today I have become your Father" (Hebrews 1:5, citing Psalm 2:7). The same goes for 2 Samuel 7:14's use of "Father" and "Son," where the original text was about David and Israel's God. Dramatically, the Instructor reshapes a passage about angels worshiping God to a line about angels worshiping the

Son (Hebrews 1:6, citing Deuteronomy 32:43). With a subtle move the Instructor writes "The One who makes" (*Second Testament*) instead of "He" (NIV) in 1:7, and this "One" is the Son. The angels are created; the Son is Creator.

Five Truths about Jesus in Hebrews

The sermon sets forth five elemental truths about the life and ministry of Jesus:

1. His humanity relates him fully to all humans.
2. His exemplary sonship is a model and means of hope for all.
3. His life and death afford us access to God.
4. He now holds a continuing priesthood.
5. His present ministry as ascended Savior grants a ready and necessary help to all who call upon him.

Massey-Kaalund, "Hebrews," 472.

The angels are temporary beings (Hebrews 1:7), "either with the gentleness of a breeze or the intensity of a flame" (Peeler, *Hebrews*, 60). But God's Son occupies an eternal throne (1:8–9, citing Psalm 45:6–7). This citation has a bonus element. The Instructor calls the Son (Jesus) "O God," and the whole citation only makes sense about the Son if the Son is God. Making sense of how it works requires concentration. The Instructor's point is subtle because the first use of *God* in "therefore God, your God" refers to the Son while the second ("your [the Son's] God" refers to God the Father!) Hebrews 1:10 connects the term *Lord* back to the term *God* in 1:8, which means the Son is called the Lord, and the Lord of verse ten is the creator and the endless, unchanging sustainer of life. As the angels were lower in rank because they are temporary (1:7), so in verse thirteen the Instructor teaches us that God never told any angel to sit down next to him at his right hand "until I make *your* enemies a footstool for *your* feet" (emphasis added). However, God does this for the Son, indicating his eternal rule in the kingdom.

Today's reading is laced tightly with affirmations about the Son as divine and as the center of all creation. We would do well to reread 1:1–4 before and after reading 1:5–14. That opening passage to Hebrews helps us to see why the Instructor used such exalted terms for the Son-Word of God.

The Angels Rank
Below the Son

Our previous reading (1:1–4) ended on a theme the Instructor develops at length in today's reading (1:5–14). The Son's *name* ("Son") is superior to the angels, and that indicates that the *Son* is essentially superior to them. Today's reading develops this in two ways. First, the Son is eternal while the angels are temporal beings. They are but "winds" or "spirits" (same Greek word, *pneuma*), and they are but "flames of fire" (1:7). Second, the angels are sent out on mission by God to planet Earth, but once they return, they enter back into the proper stations. When the Son returned to the Throne Room of God, with his mission of purification complete (1:3), he sat down at the right hand of God as the one who inherited "all things" (1:2).

I've never been tempted to worship angels, but first century Christians were. We find such a temptation in Colosse (Colossians 2:18), and maybe the Instructor knew of the same temptation. His desire to make them inferior to Jesus could well indicate some were ranking angels alongside or above Jesus. We might ponder what ranks alongside or even above

Jesus for us. Did God, we could ask, ever ask *wealth* or *sex* or *alcohol* or *appearance* or *homes* or *career* or *knowledge* or *fame* or *clothing* to sit down at his right hand? Only Jesus deserves our adoration and total affection. What is temporary, what wears out, what dies, what fluctuates, what is undependable, and what evaporates can never occupy a central place in our hearts. Pursue things that last, he instructs them, where God, the Eternal One, is (cf. Hebrews 10:34; 11:16; 13:14).

The theme of a long faithfulness belongs in our reflection: If this is the Son who has redeemed us, and if this Son is the eternal God who creates, sustains, redeems, and rules from the Throne Room, then we not only have the power of God in us and with us, but we have the capacities to be those noted by a long faithfulness. As Gareth Cockerill says so well, "God's address to the Son on the occasion of his enthronement is ever-present. The Son continues to be the eternal, incarnate, exalted Son at God's right hand *who is fully adequate to meet his people's need*" (Cockerill, *Hebrews*, 5).

QUESTIONS FOR REFLECTION AND APPLICATION

1. In what ways do you notice God speaking through the Bible?

2. What does it mean for Jesus to be both fully God and God's Son?

3. How much does your knowledge of the Bible and ability to quote it relate to your frequency of reading?

4. How many times (if any) have you read the Bible all the way through? (No shame regardless of your answer!) Does this study section make you want to know the Bible more by reading it more?

5. How do you approach studying the Bible? What tools and resources do you use?

FOR FURTHER READING

Kevin Vanhoozer, *Mere Christian Hermeneutics: Transfiguring What It Means to Read the Bible Theologically* (Grand Rapids: Zondervan Academic, 2024).

AN EXHORTATION TO LONG FAITHFULNESS #1

Hebrews 2:1–4

¹ We must pay the most careful attention, therefore, to what we have heard, so that we do not drift away. ² For since the message spoken through angels was binding, and every violation and disobedience received its just punishment, ³ how shall we escape if we ignore so great a salvation? This salvation, which was first announced by the Lord, was confirmed to us by those who heard him. ⁴ God also testified to it by signs, wonders and various miracles, and by gifts of the Holy Spirit distributed according to his will.

Few are the Christians who, in being confronted with the strong words of today's reading, are not troubled by their implications. Many have asked: *Can I lose my salvation?* Many answer back with: *No, God is faithful, and he has promised to keep me securely.* But then they read these verses, or other verses like them, and they return to that first question. That answer can seem assuring to those whose attention gets stirred by the words of the exhortation. There are five such warning passages in this Sermon. Whether or not a person can walk away from their final redemption or not, the warning passages have accomplished their task over the centuries: They grab our attention, they lead to deeper introspection, and they exhort us to a long faithfulness.

Their purpose is not to scare the innards out of us. Their purpose is to exhort and to then press upon us a strong warning. That is, they exhort us to a long faithfulness but simultaneously warn us of the dangers of hopping off the path to return to the world. The possibility of leaving the path is real, as the wilderness generation proved (cf. 3:7–4:13). But the Instructor doesn't mention anyone who has made that choice. In our reflections on the five warning passages, we will develop one theme per passage (see sidebar: "The Warning Passages of Hebrews: Themes," p. 31).

DRIFTING AWAY

The Instructor seemingly jumps ahead to a concern that has not become apparent to us, though his audience surely knew that this Sermon would cause a stir. Congregations know such things. The mood is in the air before the first word is uttered. He urges them to "pay the most careful attention" to the gospel message and the need for a long faithfulness (2:1). Paying attention, or absorbing one's attention (*Second Testament*), prevents drifting away the way a boat unmoors from a dock and slowly finds its way into the unknown depths of the sea. The Instructor will use an anchor as the image of what secures the believer to the dock of redemption (6:19). The Instructor "fears that they might 'drift away' little by little from fatigue, inconvenience, indifference, distraction, peer pressure, social exclusion, and/or growing persecution" (Cockerill, *Hebrews*, 11).

He stiffens his instruction with an *a fortiori* argument: If the "message spoken through angels," that is, the law of

Moses (Galatians 3:19–20; Acts 7:30, 38, 53), was "binding" and received just consequences for violations, the message of the Son will be *all the more binding with all the greater consequences* (2:2–3). We have sentimentalized angels into cute figurines, but we need this reminder from Kathleen Norris: "The angels of scripture have an admirable self-possession. 'Fear not' is what they always urge of the humans they encounter. But the angels populating the card, gift, and hobby shops of American malls suggest that there is nothing at all to fear" (Norris, *Amazing Grace*, 328). She's right. The words they spoke to humans instilled the fear, or awe, of God. The violation of violations in the biblical story was the golden calf story (Exodus 32), and Hebrews will turn its attention in chapters three and four to the wilderness generation's struggles. The exhortation in today's reading, then, is a "warning about what is lost by those who, having heard the message about salvation, selfishly and faithlessly 'drift away' from it" (Massey-Kaalund, "Hebrews," 474).

To anticipate what comes next in our reflection, the Instructor reminds this first generation after Jesus of what they have received by God's grace: "this salvation . . . was confirmed to us by those who heard him [Jesus] . . . [and confirmed] by signs, wonders and various miracles, and by gifts of the Holy Spirit" (2:3–4). The believers who heard this Sermon immediately recalled the glorious powers of redemption they had seen when the gospel took root in their community of faith. We ought here to remind ourselves that this message of salvation in Christ ties back to the Son-Word of God who is God incarnate, the redeemer and purifier, and the one destined to rule all creation. Those who affirm the truths about Jesus and who had experienced this redemption could recall their own stories: *I remember when Sarah's daughter was healed, and I did see the conversion of a total household and they are with us today,* and *Publius has become an amazing gospel agent in our community, and no one would have expected him to become such a gifted person.* Such were the kinds of stories they immediately recalled when they heard the words *was confirmed to us.*

The Warning Passages of Hebrews: Themes

1. 2:1–4 ("We have" and "Because we have")
2. 3:7–4:13 (Audience)
3. 5:11–6:12 (Sin)
4. 10:19–39 (Consequences)
5. 12:4–29 (Pastoral Care)

Not all agree that #5 is a separable warning passage.

For an extensive discussion comparing views of the warning passages in Hebrews, see Herbert W. Bateman IV, editor, *Four Views on the Warning Passages in Hebrews* (Grand Rapids: Kregel, 2007). The four authors of the views are Grant R. Osborne, Buist M. Fanning, Gareth Lee Cockerill, and Randall C. Gleason.

David deSilva reminds us of two themes we need to keep constantly in mind when we read these warning passages, and he introduces the book of Hebrews with these two themes: *What we have* and *Because of what we have* (deSilva, *Hebrews,* 9–13). Our passage not only reveals this "we have / because we have" pattern of thinking; it opens with "Because this is true" (2:1; *Second Testament*; NIV delays the "therefore"). The truth is what God said about and to the Son in chapter one, and that truth will expand throughout this Sermon. Let's look at both of deSilva's themes.

WE HAVE . . .

Here are the gifts *we have* because of God's gracious redemption in Christ: (1) a great high priest (4:14; 8:1); (2) a hold on the hope set before us, which encourages us (6:18); (3) a hope "as an anchor for the soul, firm and secure" (6:19); (4) "confidence to enter the Most Holy Place by the blood of Jesus" (10:19); (5) "better and lasting possessions" (10:34); (6) "such a great cloud of witnesses" (12:1); and (7) "an altar from which" no others may partake (13:10).

We have the Priest of all priests, the hope of all hopes, access of all accesses, possessions that outlive all possessions, witnesses around us in abundance, and an altar for us alone. We have God with us and for us, we have redemption and empowerment, we have myriads in our community, and we have all this for all eternity. All because of God's sending the Son to purify access for us to God. All of this is a gift, all is grace. The Creator, Sustainer, Redeemer Son-Word of God is on our side, and he is altogether capable and sufficient to handle our case before God. This is what *we have*, and . . .

. . . BECAUSE WE HAVE . . .

Because of this multitude of graces, and in spite of the cost of a long faithfulness—because of what we have, we are called to that long faithfulness. The Instructor reminds his congregation of their agency and choice to walk away or to walk on the path of a long faithfulness. The path is paved by Christ, the pioneer (2:10; 12:2), and our energies to walk derive from God's empowering strength, but we must choose to walk on that path by drawing the strength needed from God. "Great gifts call for great gratitude" (deSilva, *Hebrews*, 11). Gift-giving in the ancient world entailed a kind of reception that prompted relationship and reciprocation. So, as deSilva reminds us, because we have these gifts: (1) We are to approach God's throne of grace with confidence (4:14, 16); (2) we are to draw near, hold on, not neglect fellowship, and encourage (10:19–25); and (3) we are to be thankful (12:28). Each of these begins with a *because-we-have* and leads to our agency and choice to walk the path of a long faithfulness. As Eugene Peterson once wrote, "We cannot take a word of Jesus here and think on it for a few minutes, then admire and act there. This is a world-determining and life-transforming person we are involved with. No detail of our lives is exempt from his energetic, eternal work" (Peterson, *On Living Well*, 90).

Notice how the Instructor shapes his warnings. He does not teach them any special methods. He does not provide insider information. He does not suggest positive thinking. He does not ignore human responsibility. He does not offer fake or false assurances. He does not appeal to inner disciplines, to personal giftedness, or to human ingenuity. He does not urge them to look around at the life of others and take note that we are no worse than the others. He goes straight to God's abundant, magnificent, and utterly sufficient redeeming grace, *and because of that grace*, the Instructor exhorts and warns believers to a long faithfulness.

Long faithfulness requires personal formation over time. We grow individually in God's grace through the spiritual disciplines of routine prayer, Bible reading, sufficient solitude to hear God speak to us, fellowship with others, at times perhaps spiritual direction, growing in our understanding of ourselves that at times requires a therapist, and routine reflection on where we have been, where we are, and where we need to go. We are on a journey from here to the Rest, and one element of developing an assurance in our walk is to spend time in the presence of God. (We will develop other themes of this long faithfulness in other reflections.)

QUESTIONS FOR REFLECTION
AND APPLICATION

1. What might cause people to drift away from God?

2. How do God's multitude of graces (gifts) prompt us to reciprocally give to God our faithfulness?

3. Look up Galatians 3:19–20 and Acts 7:30, 38, 53. What do you notice about angels and the law of Moses?

4. How have you seen God's redemption confirmed to you in the lives of those around you?

5. Do you have stories from your first days of faith that were glowing evidence of the work of God in your midst?

FOR FURTHER READING

Kathleen Norris, *Amazing Grace: A Vocabulary of Faith* (New York: Riverhead, 1998).

Eugene Peterson, *On Living Well: Brief Reflections on Wisdom for Walking in the Way of Jesus* (Colorado Springs: WaterBrook, 2021).

THE PIONEER OF
LONG FAITHFULNESS

Hebrews 2:5–18

⁵ It is not to angels that he has subjected the world to come, about which we are speaking. ⁶ But there is a place where someone has testified:

> "What is mankind that you are mindful of them,
>   a son of man that you care for him?
> ⁷ You made them a little lower than the angels;
>   you crowned them with glory and honor
>   ⁸ and put everything under their feet."

In putting everything under them, God left nothing that is not subject to them. Yet at present we do not see everything subject to them. ⁹ But we do see Jesus, who was made lower than the angels for a little while, now crowned with glory and honor because he suffered death, so that by the grace of God he might taste death for everyone.

¹⁰ In bringing many sons and daughters to glory, it was fitting that God, for whom and through whom everything exists, should make the pioneer of their salvation perfect through what he suffered. ¹¹ Both the one who makes people holy and those who are made

holy are of the same family. So Jesus is not ashamed to call them brothers and sisters.

¹² *He says,*

> *"I will declare your name to my brothers and sisters;*
> *in the assembly I will sing your praises."*

¹³ *And again,*

> *"I will put my trust in him."*

And again he says,

> *"Here am I, and the children God has given me."*

¹⁴ *Since the children have flesh and blood, he too shared in their humanity so that by his death he might break the power of him who holds the power of death—that is, the devil—*¹⁵ *and free those who all their lives were held in slavery by their fear of death.* ¹⁶ *For surely it is not angels he helps, but Abraham's descendants.* ¹⁷ *For this reason he had to be made like them, fully human in every way, in order that he might become a merciful and faithful high priest in service to God, and that he might make atonement for the sins of the people.* ¹⁸ *Because he himself suffered when he was tempted, he is able to help those who are being tempted.*

D o you recall reading the story about the five daughters of Zelophehad? Their story straddles two chapters in the Old Testament book we call Numbers (26–27). As parcels of land were being allocated to families, the daughters of a deceased man named Zelophehad,* from the tribe of Manasseh (son of Joseph), came forward with a legal petition.

---

* Pronounced "Tzeloph-uh-kad" or "Tzeloph-kad."

Standing before all the notables, these five women demanded a change in the law. Their hope appears as a good, moral question: "Why should our father's name disappear from his clan because he had no son? Give us property among our father's relatives." Moses had the reputation of being nothing if not fair and just as a judge. No law on the books covered the situation of these daughters. Instead of devising a law himself, out of humility Moses went directly to YHWH (Yahweh). Since he was on intimate terms with God, YHWH told Moses to allocate the land to the women. Because of their courage, insight, and rightful perception of justice, God reveals to Moses a new set of laws:

> If a man dies and leaves no son, give his inheritance to his daughter.
> If he has no daughter, give his inheritance to his brothers.
> If he has no brothers, give his inheritance to his father's brothers.
> If his father had no brothers, give his inheritance to the nearest relative in his clan, that he may possess it.
> This is to have the force of law for the Israelites, as the LORD commanded Moses. (Numbers 27:8–11)

A precedent was set that would establish the right for a daughter to inherit her father's property—for all time. This precedent made these five women *pioneers* in the history of Israel's laws.

Lilian Bland was the first woman to fly an airplane; Amelia Earhart was the first woman to fly solo across the Atlantic Ocean; Betty Miller was the first woman across the Pacific Ocean; Jerrie Mock was the first woman to fly solo around the world; Jacqueline Cochran was the first woman to break the sound barrier, and Emily Howell Warner was the first woman to become an American airline captain. All because Raymonde de Laroche was the first woman to earn a pilot's license. Raymonde was the *pioneer* of women pioneer pilots (Wikipedia). Pioneers carve pathways for followers, forming paths that become busy highways.

Jesus, like the five daughters and Raymonde de Laroche, was a *pioneer* for you and for me to travel the path of a long faithfulness that leads to our final salvation (Hebrews 2:10). Because this Sermon proceeds in a special way, I want to set our passage in its context. Our previous passage, Hebrews 2:1–4, was an interruption, or a moment of pastoral exhortation, or a bridge to today's reading. Notice that once again we meet up with comparisons of Jesus to angels (2:5–9), showing us that 1:5 continued at least through 2:9. To complete this picture, those angels are going to show up one more time at 2:16. Thus the larger context extends to the end of chapter two. (By the way, I prefer to think of 2:1–4 as a moment of pastoral exhortation. The Instructor needed to get this exhortation in before he uttered another word about Jesus and the angels.) Today's passage, then, is in the heart of a comparison of Jesus to the angels, and Jesus is better. What's more is that because Jesus is so much better, he has carved a path for us. We can follow in his steps, and as we follow him step by step, we discover the life of a long faithfulness.

JESUS AND ANGELS

God sets the order for this world and the world to come. Angels were created to be divine messengers for the sake of humans (1:14). They have not been chosen to rule this or the next world. The Son of God will be the ruler. The NIV, I believe, mistakenly translates 2:6–8, conveying the message that the Old Testament selection is about humans in general, and therefore us, and therefore about humans ruling the world. Notice these words that expand what the text says: "mankind" and "them" (2:6), then two more uses of "them" in verse seven with a "their" in verse eight. Again, the NIV has "them" twice at the end of verse eight (after citing Psalm 8). This suggests humans are in view. They are not. These verses are about the Son of God, who represents all humans, or "everyone" (cf. 2:9). Each of these terms is singular in Greek: It is a "human" (not "mankind"), and it is "a son of man" and thus the "them's" are either a "he" or a "one" (as in *Second Testament*). I suggest this correction because the Instructor intentionally transforms this psalm into one about Jesus. By the way, did you notice that the Instructor knew that Bible verse from Psalm 8:4–6 but couldn't cite "chapter and verse"? So, he wrote "someone somewhere" (Hebrews 2:6; *Second Testament*). These verses are about the incarnation of the Son of God, not about the condition of all humans. As the fully representative human, Jesus stands in for each of us. As Madison Pierce writes, "Jesus is a perfect representative of every individual person, not just every category of person" (Pierce, "Hebrews," 587).

Verse nine's "But [or, So] we do see Jesus" begins to introduce some new information about Jesus. The Instructor, with a rhetorically deft move, shifts from the invisibility of the Son's future rule to the visibility of the present rule of Jesus as the Ascended and Sitting One. He became incarnate in a condition "lower than the angels" but "only for a little while." At the present, he is "crowned with glory and honor" (2:9). That's the present state for Jesus. How he got there is why he is the Pioneer. The Instructor informs us of what preceded his elevation: "because he suffered death." As readers of the Gospels, we know the facts of Jesus' life. We know about his birth, his public ministry, the conflicts in his life, and we know he was brutally crucified. It was because he lived a long faithfulness to the Father that the Son's death was overturned with resurrection and ascension to the right hand of God. He was thus made "perfect through what he suffered" (2:10). For Jesus to be perfected does not impute sin to Jesus. Instead, "perfection" is the Instructor's term for Jesus having completed the mission of his long faithfulness. This story was never told of angels.

Let's jump down the passage to discover something more about angels. Not only are the angels destined to play second (or third, or fourth) fiddle to Jesus, but they are not redeemed as humans can be and are (2:16). The term for redemption here is "helps" (NIV), but a more literal rendering is that Jesus "doesn't take hold of envoys [angels] but he takes hold of Abra'am's seed" (*Second Testament*). The image conveyed is the Son of God taking hold of us, hand in hand, to lead us onward on the path to the kingdom of God. Jesus was also not made like the angels. In his incarnation Jesus was made like humans (2:17). We are not destined to be angels because we are not in the line of angels. We are destined to become Christlike because we are made in the image of God, and the pure image of God is Jesus (Romans 8:29; 1 Corinthians 15:49; 2 Corinthians 3:18; 4:4; Colossians 1:15; 3:10).

SIBLINGS AND JESUS

The path of long faithfulness for Jesus entered the dark tunnel of death, but he died "to taste death for everyone" (2:9). The emphasis of the Instructor will not fall on Good Friday. Death is something Jesus went "through" (2:10). It was a delay in his journey from the Father to earth and through death to emerge from the darkness into the light of resurrection and ascension. Because he tasted death for you and me, he is able to lead "many siblings to splendor" (*Second Testament*). The atonement for the Instructor transcends the transactions of the cross to include being exalted to be with the Son and God in glory so he can sit down as the one whose task was perfected.

An amazing statement deserves attention: "Both the One who makes people holy and those who are made holy are of the same family" (2:11). The Greek does not have "family" here; it has only "are all from one" (*Second Testament*). That is, they are now of and from the same divine life, and the NIV's paraphrase, "same family," expresses this well. Jesus, because of his incarnation, "is not ashamed," or his status is not lowered, when he calls them "siblings" (2:12; *Second Testament*), which the Instructor supports by appealing to three Scriptures (Psalm 22:22, Isaiah 8:17, and 8:18).

Two features stand out in these citations: First, that Jesus is the one speaking (2:11–12). God speaks Scriptures in chapter one and *the Son speaks scriptures in chapter two*. Some call 2:12–13 the speech of Jesus. Second, notice "I will be persuaded in him" (*Second Testament*), which in the NIV is "I will put my trust in him" (Hebrews 2:13). There it is: The Instructor sees Jesus as the Pioneer in that he, too, was persuaded about who God is and what God has promised and so trusted in him. This trust led him both into the tunnel of darkness and straight through it into Easter's resurrection and the Ascension Day's exaltation. As Massey and Kaalund said, "The writer thus accents attention upon Jesus as religious *subject* in order to highlight the importance of Jesus as religious *object*. In so doing, the writer's insight into the human experience of Jesus accents his obedience in pilgrimage; it shows him as a figure of hope for those who look to him as the worthy 'pioneer of their deliverance'" (Massey-Kaalund, "Hebrews," 474).

Our passage teaches us to value the incarnation and the ascension along with the crucifixion and resurrection. Without the incarnation, there is no redemption (2:9, 11, 14–15), and that is why the Instructor informs his congregants that Jesus "shared in their humanity" (2:14). As Massey and Kaalund say it, "The message about Jesus in Hebrews is that he is a Savior fully identified with us by a common humanity and by raw experience" (Massey-Kaalund, "Hebrews," 472). Because he suffered, which began with identifying with us in body, he was able to "break the power of him who holds the power of death—that is, the devil—and free those who all their lives were held in slavery by their fear of death" (2:14–15, with 2:17). American evangelicalism is not the only group of Christians that so emphasizes the cross that it neglects what happens on either side: incarnation and ascension. Raise your hand if that is true about you. (My hand is raised.)

As one "fully human in every way," he is able to become "a mercy-giving and allegiant Senior Priest" (2:17, *Second Testament*). He knows us. He's been where we have been, where we are, and where we will go. He has been tempted and tested as we are tempted and tested (2:18). These are words once again of Jesus' being the Pioneer of our redemption and perfection. If we keep our eyes on Jesus (12:2), we will see him in the darkness and in the light, in the turns and the dips and the climbs, and in the footprints left on the path as we look down. We are called to a long faithfulness. But what we are really called to is to keep our eyes on Jesus because he's the Pioneer and Perfecter of the long faithfulness.

QUESTIONS FOR REFLECTION AND APPLICATION

1. How does Jesus serve as a pioneer for our faithfulness?

2. What does "perfection" mean to the Instructor?

3. Why do you think God made Jesus like humans and not like the angels in his incarnation?

4. Why are Jesus' incarnation and ascension as important to the gospel as his crucifixion and resurrection?

5. What does it mean to you to know that Jesus has been tempted and tested just as you are?

FOR FURTHER READING

Wikipedia about women firsts in aviation: https://en.wikipedia.org/wiki/List_of_women%27s_firsts.

AN EXHORTATION TO LONG FAITHFULNESS #2 PART ONE

Hebrews 3:1–19

[1] *Therefore, holy brothers and sisters, who share in the heavenly calling, fix your thoughts on Jesus, whom we acknowledge as our apostle and high priest.* [2] *He was faithful to the one who appointed him, just as Moses was faithful in all God's house.* [3] *Jesus has been found worthy of greater honor than Moses, just as the builder of a house has greater honor than the house itself.* [4] *For every house is built by someone, but God is the builder of everything.* [5] *"Moses was faithful as a servant in all God's house," bearing witness to what would be spoken by God in the future.* [6] *But Christ is faithful as the Son over God's house. And we are his house, if indeed we hold firmly to our confidence and the hope in which we glory.*

[7] *So, as the Holy Spirit says:*

> *"Today, if you hear his voice,*
> [8] *do not harden your hearts*
> *as you did in the rebellion,*
> *during the time of testing in the wilderness,*
> [9] *where your ancestors tested and tried me,*

> though for forty years they saw what I did.
> ¹⁰ That is why I was angry with that generation;
> I said, 'Their hearts are always going astray,
> and they have not known my ways.'
> ¹¹ So I declared on oath in my anger,
> 'They shall never enter my rest.'"

¹² See to it, brothers and sisters, that none of you has a sinful, unbelieving heart that turns away from the living God. ¹³ But encourage one another daily, as long as it is called "Today," so that none of you may be hardened by sin's deceitfulness. ¹⁴ We have come to share in Christ, if indeed we hold our original conviction firmly to the very end.

¹⁵ As has just been said:

> "Today, if you hear his voice,
> do not harden your hearts
> as you did in the rebellion."

¹⁶ Who were they who heard and rebelled? Were they not all those Moses led out of Egypt? ¹⁷ And with whom was he angry for forty years? Was it not with those who sinned, whose bodies perished in the wilderness? ¹⁸ And to whom did God swear that they would never enter his rest if not to those who disobeyed? ¹⁹ So we see that they were not able to enter, because of their unbelief.

When reading stories about the children of Israel—their exodus from Egypt, their receiving the law of Moses at Mount Sinai, their wanderings in the wilderness, their entry into the land of promise—I find myself welcomed in their company. That is, I find myself being one of the children of Israel. I participate in what the exodus must have been like, what the crossing of the Red Sea must have felt like on the feet, what the dusty wilderness must have done to the body and face and clothing daily, what it was like to hear Moses read those Ten Commandments, what it was like to stand on the eastern side of the Jordan River, believing that land was destined for me and my family . . . and then I open my eyes, and I'm sitting right here in my basement library. Thousands of miles from Egypt and Saudi Arabia and the modern State of Israel.

Imagined participation in that history is what it means to be a faithful Bible reader. Which means, too, that I need to participate in the strong words of the psalmist (95:7–11) that evoke the days of Moses on the cusp of entering into the promised land (Numbers 14), and also in today's reading in Hebrews, with its loud, strong word *Today* (Hebrews 3:7). Today's reading is the second warning passage in Hebrews (2:1–4; 3:7–4:13; 5:11–6:12; 10:19–39; 12:4–29). Each warning passage has four elements: the audience, the sin that can be committed, the exhortation to turn away from committing that sin, and the consequences for those who do commit that sin (see sidebar: "Four Elements of the Warning Passages," below). For readers of this Sermon (and remember, this is at least a Sermon-like communication from the Instructor to a congregation or audience), since each warning passage has each of those four elements, each of those elements can be studied topically to create a composite picture. In today's reflection, we will draw a composite picture of the audience to begin the reflection.

Four Elements of the Warning Passages

1. The audience
2. The sin
3. The exhortation
4. The consequences of the sin

THE AUDIENCE

Again, I will compose a sketch of the audience of this Sermon by isolating the specific terms about the audience in all of the warning passages. At times the Instructor includes himself in the audience. We should not dismiss this as simply rhetorical empathy, as if a teacher were to say to her class, "We're having a hard time with this passage, aren't we?" The students know she's not, and she knows she's not, but she does it anyway to sound empathetic. The Instructor is not pretending. He's one of them. Notice the use of "we" at 3:14: "*We* have come to share in Christ, if indeed we hold *our* original conviction firmly to the end." Today's reading is followed in the first verse of chapter four with another "we": "Therefore, since the promise of entering his rest still stands, let *us* be careful that none of *you* be found to have fallen short of it." But notice the shift from "we" to "you" in that verse. At 4:11 we read something like 4:1: "Let *us*, therefore, make every effort to enter that rest, so that *no one* will perish by following their example of disobedience."

At times, the Instructor calls the audience his (spiritual) siblings ("brothers" in Greek), and in today's passage he does this at 3:12, which we quote: "See to it, brothers and sisters, that none of you has a sinful heart." The Instructor thinks of his congregation as siblings in Christ (see also 3:1; 10:19; 13:22). The instance at 3:1 is worth noticing more carefully because of their spiritual relationship to him and to Christ is clear: "Therefore, holy brothers and sisters, who share in the heavenly calling." At 2:11, 12, and 17, the brothers and sisters have been made holy, and Jesus calls them his siblings for whom he has made atonement. At 10:29 he sees the audience as those who have been "sanctified." Most important is 4:3, and I will quote my more literal translation: "For we, the allegiant [faithful, believing] ones, enter into the resting place." The NIV translates: "We who have believed." Here, the Instructor names his audience as believers, and that is why he can recount their conversion days (2:3–4; see, too, 6:10; 10:22, 32–34). They are, in other words, his "beloved" (6:9; NIV has "dear friends").

I now want to summarize what we find in this Sermon in a little more systematic categories: The Instructor knew that his audience had made a credible confession of the Christian faith, they showed evidence of maturation in the faith, the Holy Spirit had worked in and through them, and they knew the powers of the age to come in their experience. The Instructor saw them as his siblings in Christ. That is, he thought of them as fellow believers, as those who had been saved. No wonder, then, that we can identify with the children of Israel in their exodus and wanderings to the Jordan River, but such identification includes receiving the "Today" warning as one for us too.

PONDER JESUS FIRST

The Instructor knows it is all too easy to begin pondering ourselves—how deep and wide and high our faith is—and seeking to convince ourselves that we are among the elect, that we are saved, and that we are "safe and secure from all alarms" (E. A. Hoffman, "Leaning on the Everlasting Arms"). But that old hymn, which my home church as a child sang with gusto, points us to exactly what the Instructor did as well. Here is where he begins this warning passage: "Therefore . . . fix your thoughts on Jesus, whom we acknowledge as our apostle and high priest," because he was "faithful" to God and "found worthy of greater honor than Moses" because he was "faithful as the *Son* over God's house" (3:1–5). The distinguishing mark of Jesus here is his faithfulness to the even greater task than that given to Moses, who was an "attendant"

(3:2, 6; *Second Testament*). Plus, Moses was an attendant "in" God's house; Jesus is the Son "over" God's house (3:5, 6). Before the Instructor disturbs their assumed comfort, he makes the first thing the first thing. The Instructor enters the Christian faith through the portal of who Jesus is and what he does (Christology). He maintains that portal for how he understands the Christian life (ponder Jesus first). To remind ourselves of what was said at 2:1–4, "we have . . . because we have." We have a responsibility because we have the power to accomplish that responsibility, and the power is from God.

Here Jesus is the Apostle, which means the one sent from God to us, and he is the High Priest, which means he knows us, he participates with us, he empathizes with us, and in his priestly work he both purifies us and carries us before the throne of God's grace (2:14–18; 4:14–16). As Apostle and High Priest, he is also the Pioneer (2:10). Put together, we are to ponder the Jesus of the long faithfulness who came to us to lead us on, and who also empathizes and redeems us so we can endure the long faithfulness. Many of us have stumbled over these warning passages because we get trapped in the feedback loop of pondering whether or not we are good enough, whether we have done enough, and whether we have truly and authentically believed. We can get trapped into wondering if we are self-deceived and if we might be among those who actually have an inauthentic faith that may soon wash out. Pondering ourselves, then, is a problem. The Instructor knows we are to ponder Jesus, not ourselves. He has come to us, he has carved a path through sin and evil, through the tunnel of darkness, and he has come out on the far side into the light of all lights—and he has shown us the way. All we can do is ponder Jesus and put one foot into the next footprint Jesus has left for us to follow. The Instructor's instruction emerges from his warning: "Hold firmly to our confidence and the hope in which we glory" (3:6). That word *confidence* can be translated as "boldness" or "frankness," and it describes a person who has the courage to do what is right, or to live out a long faithfulness.

OUR RESPONSE FOLLOWS PONDERING JESUS

The Instructor has created a template for his congregations' situation. He takes them (and us) back to the children of Israel in the wilderness. There the people of God sinned, their faith folded up, their feet lost their way, and their former faithfulness fell short. What the psalmist said of them are words the Instructor uses for the believers to whom he writes this Sermon. God the Father speaks in chapter one, the Son speaks in chapter two, and here in chapter three the Holy Spirit speaks (3:7 and 3:15 by implication, which becomes "God" speaking in 4:3, 5, and 7). If you follow the words here you will see that the Holy Spirit accompanied the children of Israel on their journey (Pierce, "Hebrews," 587–588). May the Spirit's words become words for us today, and may the Spirit journey with us as well.

May our *aim* of life be to enter into the rest (3:11, 18, 19; also 3:14). The rest for the children of Israel, one can presume, was not heaven or the kingdom of God but the promised land. Yet, the psalmist lives centuries later than the wilderness generation, and his "Today" was for his day as it is for our "Today" as well. As the children of Israel were exemplary, in a negative way, for the psalmist's day, so they are for the congregants hearing this Sermon. They did not enter the rest, and that non-entry becomes a metaphor for failing to reach the ultimate goal of life (see sidebar: "The Rest," pp. 58–59).

TODAY

May we become increasingly aware that our *time* is "Today" (3:7, 15). There is a profound and at times discomforting urgency about the words of the psalmist that are used by the Instructor. We need to face the summons to a long faithfulness today, as the wilderness generation faced their challenge near the end of the journey to the promised land. Neither the psalmist's nor the Instructor's immediate fear is dying. Their urgency reflects their belief that what we do today impacts who we are and how we will live tomorrow. Massey and Kaalund have observed the effects of sin on our lives: "Though [the wilderness generation] succeeded at sinning, the gains were fleshly and destructive. The gains of sin are always deadly, making the disobedient losers" (Massey-Kaalund, "Hebrews," 477). Divine judgment, which here shows up as being "hardened" (3:13), loomed over the wilderness generation and the psalmist's audience, just as it does for the Instructor, but that divine judgment can, like Romans 1:18–32, work itself out over time as a person drifts away (Hebrews 2:1–4).

Today, then, is a day for us to fight for peace in our world because peace is the path for those who follow Jesus. Long faithfulness entails not just personal communion with God. To be faithful to God on the journey toward the Rest means that we do God's will as it presents itself in our life. For instance, one of the Bible's themes for both God's future kingdom and God's people in the present moment is *peace*. Those who walk faithfully on the path behind Jesus pursue peace as Jesus himself pursued peace. We do this in our families, in our neighborhoods, in our communities, in our workplaces, in our churches, and in our nation. We seek not the shallow peace of pretending we are one or that avoids telling the truth, but instead pursue the peace that follows genuine transparency and honesty with one another. At times, transparency generates pain and wounds. Genuine peace only occurs when transparency leads to openness, repentance, transformation over time, and then harmony. Faking peace has been a characteristic of too many churches. Jesus calls us to a genuine peace. The USA is at odds with itself these days, and peacemakers on the journey to the Rest recognize the reality of the tensions. They don't suggest, "Let's all just get along." They listen, they discuss, they debate, and they discover honest differences. Some can't handle sitting at the table following such honesty; others can. Christians on the path of following Jesus desire peace and will work for that, even if it takes time away from one another as yet more time is spent at the table. Today is a time for peace for pilgrims on the path.

Like that generation, may we perceive that the *danger* is "rebellion" (3:8), but that term encircles a set of terms describing the drift and disaster of the wilderness generation. The term *rebellion* could be translated "argument" (*Second Testament*; cf. 3:16), which reflects how the children of Israel were disputing God and God's ways in Numbers 14. They chose their own way and not God's. In our passage we see the following terms inside that term: They "tried me," "going astray," not knowing the ways of God, a "sinful, unbelieving heart that turns away from the living God," participating in "sin's deceitfulness, and that they "sinned" and "disobeyed" (3:17, 18). May we all receive the *exhortation* as a call to a long faithfulness, which shows up negatively in "do not harden your hearts" (3:8, 15) or a "sinful, unbelieving heart" (3:12), but also positively in holding on to "our original conviction firmly to the very end" (3:14; cf. 3:6). That word *if* does not toss the weight onto us. As Amy Peeler has expressed it, "This 'if,' however, is built not on the strength (or lack thereof) of human faith but on the strong foundation of Christ's faithfulness" (Peeler, *Hebrews*, 105; see comments at 2:1–4).

Faith, then, is a conversion of who we are to who God is in Christ. As Barbara Brown Taylor once wrote, "While it may seem more respectable to approach faith as an intellectual exercise or more satisfying to approach it as an emotional one, our relationship to God is not simply a matter of what we think or how we feel. It is more comprehensive than that, and more profound. It is a full-bodied relationship in which mind and heart, spirit and flesh, are converted to a new way of experiencing and responding to the world. It is the surrender of one set of images and the acceptance of another. It is a matter of learning to see the world, each other, and ourselves as God sees us, and to live as if God's reality were the only one that mattered" (Taylor, *The Preaching Life*, 44). That's the kind of faith that generates both personal transformation and social conversation.

For the children of Israel, all they needed to do was to be faithful both *at the very end* and *to the end* of their journey. "Faith for Hebrews is manifest in persons who are steadfastly dependent on God in an intimate way" (Peeler, *Hebrews*, 117). But that wilderness generation failed just before the entry, and they failed in part because they had failed so often during the wilderness journey. The Instructor compressed the future of his hearers into a moment: He wants them to see that they, like the wilderness generation, are standing at the Jordan and ready to enter the kingdom. How could we maintain this long faithfulness? By encouraging one another (3:13; 10:32–34; 13:1–3, 16) as we together hear the word of God to us because we, too, face a new "Today."

QUESTIONS FOR REFLECTION AND APPLICATION

1. What are the four elements of the warning passages?

2. Who is the possible audience of this Sermon? What can we know about the audience so far in the Sermon?

3. What does it mean for Jesus to be our High Priest?

4. What does real peace look like for Christians?

5. How does it encourage you to hear that while we have responsibilities in our faithfulness to God, we also have the power to accomplish those responsibilities?

FOR FURTHER READING

E. A. Hoffman, "Leaning on the Everlasting Arms," public domain. See: https://hymnary.org/text /what_a_fellowship_what_a_joy_divine.
Barbara Brown Taylor, *The Preaching Life* (Boston: Cowley, 1993).

AN EXHORTATION TO
LONG FAITHFULNESS #2
PART TWO

Hebrews 4:1–13

¹ *Therefore, since the promise of entering his rest still stands, let us be careful that none of you be found to have fallen short of it.* ² *For we also have had the good news proclaimed to us, just as they did; but the message they heard was of no value to them, because they did not share the faith of those who obeyed.*

³ *Now we who have believed enter that rest, just as God has said,*

> *"So I declared on oath in my anger,*
> *'They shall never enter my rest.'"*

And yet his works have been finished since the creation of the world.

⁴ *For somewhere he has spoken about the seventh day in these words: "On the seventh day God rested from all his works."* ⁵ *And again in the passage above he says, "They shall never enter my rest."*

⁶ *Therefore since it still remains for some to enter that rest, and*

since those who formerly had the good news proclaimed to them did not go in because of their disobedience,

⁷ God again set a certain day, calling it "Today." This he did when a long time later he spoke through David, as in the passage already quoted:

> *"Today, if you hear his voice,*
> *do not harden your hearts."*

⁸ For if Joshua had given them rest, God would not have spoken later about another day. ⁹ There remains, then, a Sabbath-rest for the people of God; ¹⁰ for anyone who enters God's rest also rests from their works, just as God did from his. ¹¹ Let us, therefore, make every effort to enter that rest, so that no one will perish by following their example of disobedience.

¹² For the word of God is alive and active. Sharper than any double-edged sword, it penetrates even to dividing soul and spirit, joints and marrow; it judges the thoughts and attitudes of the heart. ¹³ Nothing in all creation is hidden from God's sight. Everything is uncovered and laid bare before the eyes of him to whom we must give account.

The children of Israel neither entered nor enjoyed the original promised Rest. The promise fell apart because the people failed to obey. The original promise was delivered with an expectation, even requirement, for the children of Israel to be faithful. Covenant faithfulness reciprocates the eternal covenantal relationship God makes with all humans. Which is why the Instructor returns to Psalm 95:7–11 for more discussion, this time as an encouragement (see 3:7–19 for his first discussion of the passage): The original covenantal arrangement remains, including the promise of the Rest. The Instructor brings out one more example of how his mind works in this: The final Rest transcends the original Rest, just as the leader (Jesus) of the people transcends the original leaders (Moses and Joshua).

THE REST

The Instructor uses the term *since* three times in the NIV of today's reading to express assumed truths. The first use appears at 4:1 ("since the promise of entering his rest still stands") and the second at 4:6 repeats the first ("since it still remains for some to enter that rest") and then adds a third with ("and since those who formerly had the good news proclaimed to them . . ."). The Rest remains a promise because the former generation did not fulfill their covenant obligation. This new promised Rest, then, remains for the Instructor's audience, and by connection, it remains for us. It only exists and remains because of the "world's biggest *if*," which is found in Paul: "If Christ was raised from the dead, (1) we are witnesses of the truth, (2) our preaching is true and our faith is sound, and (3) our sin is unraveled and erased and we can be made right with God—for eternity" (based on 1 Corinthians 15:12–19, from Scot McKnight, *The Heaven Promise*, 32). That is, *if* (and *since*) Jesus was truly raised from the dead, the heaven promise, the promise of an eternal Rest, is secure and held out as an option for humans today.

The Rest

For the believers, the final, ultimate goal of this life is eternal life in the world to come (2:5) or the unshakeable kingdom of God (1:8; 12:28) or heavenly home (11:16), which is the same as the future city (13:14). Most today speak of this final goal as heaven (cf. 2:8–10; 6:19–20; 9:24), which it is, but the popular idea of heaven tends to be an immaterial world of spirits and songs rather than the new heavens and new earth coming down to earth (Revelation 20–22). The ultimate goal is about the transformation of all creation, and we are called to participate in the transformation that has already begun.

The Instructor's favorite term for this future is not "heaven" or "the kingdom," but the "Rest," a term he picked up in Psalm 95:9 ("They shall never enter my rest"). The term is used in Hebrews at 3:11, 18; 4:1, 3, 5, 6, 8, 10, 11. The Rest into which the faithful enter is God's own Sabbath (4:3–5: "my" rest; also 4:9). Madison Pierce says this so well: "This is a promise for every person to enter into this space where God has been" since he rested from his creative work (Pierce, "Hebrews," 589–590). This makes clear that the Rest is provided for those who have completed the works assigned to them (4:10). The New Testament is unafraid to call believers to a life of (good) works, and the word used in 4:10 is the plural "works" (as in the NIV). As God rested from the work of creation, so the faithful rest from their obedience.

The ultimate message in today's reading only works for those who embrace the prospect of the Rest. Many today have either lost hope for this Rest or become so preoccupied with life in this world that the Rest no longer matters to them. Comfort has a way of keeping us from pondering deeper questions about life and life after death. Others have grown snarky about the Christian belief in heaven. Their motto is "both heaven and hell can be now," and they may add, "so I concentrate on bringing heaven to earth." Such persons tend to be younger rather than older, while pastors constantly face folks who are standing at the gate as they await their number to be called to enter into what lies beyond this life. For such persons, the Rest becomes paramount. Jesus and the apostles lived for this life with another eye on the life to come. They lived with the kingdom promise daily. Jesus was the Pioneer of a long faithfulness that was not finished until he entered into that Rest (cf. 2:10; 12:2). Those who live for now with an eye on the Rest sanctify life now in ways the others don't or won't or can't.

We will all die. What happens after death? I have committed my life to trusting the vision of Jesus for the final kingdom and the message of the Instructor about the Rest. I believe in heaven because God promised to perfect us and all creation.

THE TRAGEDY

The Instructor chose a tragedy to grab his audience's attention for his warning. The wilderness generation had heard the promise of the Rest. The Instructor begins with his audience, not the old audience: "For *we* also have had the good news proclaimed to us, just as they did" (4:2), and here the good news is about the promised Rest. Instead of responding faithfully to the promise, that generation's tragedy was not "blended with allegiance" or faithfulness (*Second Testament*). At 4:1 he observed that they fell short, in 4:6 and 4:11 that they were marked by "disobedience." The tragedy meant they did not enter into the Rest. Even those who entered the land did not, according to Hebrews 4:8, enter the Rest that had been promised.

Not entering into the Rest is the tragedy of anyone who made progress in following Jesus, even for years, but chooses for any number of reasons no longer to walk in the way of Jesus (see the documentary *Once Saved, Always Saved*). For the generation of Moses and Joshua, faithfulness was measured by observance of the Torah, which corresponds in important ways with observance of the teachings of Jesus. A number of reasons are often given for why folks walk away from the faith, including the challenges of science and faith, the rational and emotional difficulties of how Christians warn about hell, difficulties found in Scripture, and the hypocrisy of Christians and fallen pastors. No matter the reasons given—and they should not be dismissed or diminished—those who walk away from the presence of Jesus, who is the center of the Christian faith, will reap the same consequence of the wilderness generation (see McKnight-Ondrey, *Finding Faith*, 7–61).

THE POSSIBILITIES

The Instructor challenges his audience with two possibilities for their future: a long faithfulness that leads to the Rest or a faithlessness that walks away. The Instructor concentrates only on his own listeners, so he has nothing to say about those who have never believed in these warning passages (though it is not hard to wonder what he might think). Since we looked at walking away already in today's reflection, I want to turn to the proper response, to long faithfulness, as explained in 4:1–13.

The NIV's "let us be careful" has a measured tone of gentleness about it, but the translations "Let us be afraid" (*Second Testament*) or "Let us fear" (Peeler, *Hebrews*, 107) are closer to the original text's meaning. The terms echo the fear of God or the awe of God in the Bible, an awe that pierces the heart with the knowledge that the God of perfections knows us, observes us, and judges us—justly. The believers are to fear lest they also "be found to have fallen short" (4:1). Believers are not to fear their enemies, but they are to have an awe for God (cf. 11:23, 26 with 4:1 and 10:31). So, I prefer thinking of the "fear of God" in terms of "awe," and to think of "fear" as a virtue (awe) misdirected. Amy Peeler points us in that direction: "When members of a community trust in God, they are appropriately fearful of the consequences of disobedience. . . . If those same members do not trust in God, however, they fall into the various manifestations of an unhealthy fear. Either they fear that their enemies are more powerful than God, or they fear that God is neither capable nor good enough to fulfill divine promises" (Peeler, *Hebrews*, 122). As the Instructor likes to remind his audience, the time for decision is narrowed to "Today" (4:7; cf. 3:7, 13, 15).

The exhortation to a long faithfulness in this warning passage appears in these words: "let us commit to enter into that resting place" (4:11; *Second Testament*). The image points us at someone who strives with effort to reach a goal. In such a life of faithfulness, believers will not "fall into the same kind of un-persuasion model" (*Second Testament*). The language, as you can sense, is distinct: It's about collapsing into a way of life that is unpersuaded to follow the path of Jesus. What can we do? James Earl Massey and Jennifer T. Kaalund offer this to their readers: "A full striving will mean staying open to God in heart and mind, with eagerness to hear God's word in order to know and do God's will" (Massey-Kaalund, "Hebrews," 477).

THE SWORD

If you have been pierced by the fierceness of the Instructor's warning, he has some clarifying words for what is going on in your heart and soul and mind and body. He makes it clear that what we feel in these warning passages is nothing less than the "word of God," by which he means (at least) Psalm 95:7–11 (cf. Hebrews 3:7–11). As Cockerill writes, the Instructor "wants us to feel in our bodies the intrusive power of God's word" (Cockerill, *Hebrews*, 35). We have felt that the word of God is "living and energetic" (*Second Testament*) and "sharper than a double-edged sword" (NIV). Because of its sharpness, a passage like Psalm 95 has the capacity to pierce "soul and spirit, joints and marrow" (Hebrews 4:12). The metaphors end there and morph into more concrete ideas: "It judges the thoughts and attitudes of the heart." If we are wobbling in our faith and wandering from the path, the word can pierce us with redemptive pain. As David deSilva says, "Submitting to God's word now about what we are committing or omitting will position us to hear God's word of affirmation and welcome in the end" (deSilva, *Hebrews*, 51).

If we think we can hide, as Adam and Eve did, we are mistaken because "there isn't a creation unapparent before God" (4:13; *Second Testament*). Everything is exposed, like the doctor's or dentist's X-rays, like a computer program's detection systems, like a mom looking into the eyes of her five-year-old. Truth be told, "everything is naked and bare-necked" (*Second Testament*) before the searching eyes of God and all will be summoned before God to "give account" (4:13).

God's sword exposes and reveals, but the intent is not judgment in the sense of damnation or even humiliation. The sword exposes even now in order for us to grow in grace, to strengthen our weakness, and to find the strength to walk in a long faithfulness. In *The Book of Common Prayer*, the weekly service begins with what is called "The Collect for Purity," and I once wrote a book echoing those words. The Collect runs like this, and I close with these words as a fitting end to today's themes:

Almighty God, to you all hearts are open, all desires
known, and from you no secrets are hid: Cleanse the
thoughts of our hearts by the inspiration of your Holy
Spirit, that we may perfectly love you, and worthily
magnify your holy name; through Christ our Lord.
Amen. (*The Book of Common Prayer,* 355)

QUESTIONS FOR REFLECTION AND APPLICATION

1. What does "Rest" mean to the Instructor?

2. Why did the Israelites not get to enter the Rest?

3. What might keep Christians today from entering the Rest?

4. How and where in your body do you experience physical reactivity when the "doubled-edged sword" of God's Word convicts you with its warnings?

5. When have you experienced warnings or convictions from God that ultimately helped you walk the path of long faithfulness?

FOR FURTHER READING

The Book of Common Prayer (New York: Oxford University Press, 1990). My book is called *To You All Hearts Are Open: Revitalizing the Church's Pattern of Asking God* (Brewster, Massachusetts: Paraclete, 2021). Amy Peeler mentions this prayer at the end of her commentary on today's reading (p. 135).

Scot McKnight, *The Heaven Promise: Engaging the Bible's Truth about Life to Come* (Colorado Springs: WaterBrook, 2015).

Scot McKnight, Hauna Ondrey, *Finding Faith, Losing Faith: Stories of Conversion and Apostasy* (Waco: Baylor University Press, 2008).

Once Saved, Always Saved https://www.youtube .com/watch?v=JVN7NXqwjro&ab_channel =OnceSavedAlwaysSaved%3FADocumentary Film.

THE HIGH PRIEST OF OUR LONG FAITHFULNESS

Hebrews 4:14–5:10

[14] Therefore, since we have a great high priest who has ascended into heaven, Jesus the Son of God, let us hold firmly to the faith we profess. [15] For we do not have a high priest who is unable to empathize with our weaknesses, but we have one who has been tempted in every way, just as we are—yet he did not sin. [16] Let us then approach God's throne of grace with confidence, so that we may receive mercy and find grace to help us in our time of need.

[5:1] Every high priest is selected from among the people and is appointed to represent the people in matters related to God, to offer gifts and sacrifices for sins. [2] He is able to deal gently with those who are ignorant and are going astray, since he himself is subject to weakness. [3] This is why he has to offer sacrifices for his own sins, as well as for the sins of the people. [4] And no one takes this honor on himself, but he receives it when called by God, just as Aaron was.

[5] In the same way, Christ did not take on himself the glory of becoming a high priest. But God said to him,

> *"You are my Son;*
> *today I have become your Father."*

⁶ And he says in another place,

> *"You are a priest forever,*
> *in the order of Melchizedek."*

⁷ During the days of Jesus' life on earth, he offered up prayers and petitions with fervent cries and tears to the one who could save him from death, and he was heard because of his reverent submission. ⁸ Son though he was, he learned obedience from what he suffered ⁹ and, once made perfect, he became the source of eternal salvation for all who obey him ¹⁰ and was designated by God to be high priest in the order of Melchizedek.

Remember, the final goal of the believer is to enter the Rest—that is, to dwell in the presence of God, in the kingdom, forever and ever. This does not diminish our time on earth. Living toward the Rest sanctifies our life, energizes it, and gives our life today ultimate perspective and direction, as well as a promised, future, final conquering of death. To get from our life today to our life in the Rest, we are called to a long faithfulness. To get to the Rest, we are to follow the Pioneer (2:10; 12:2), who, after living a life of obedience and suffering, was perfected, raised, ascended, and now sits at the right hand of God—and so becomes our Great High Priest. Jesus, then, is both our Pioneer and Priest, the Great High Priest above all high priests. He both paved the way for us and now empowers us. The emphasis in this Sermon on long faithfulness finds an even greater emphasis on the grace and power of God that makes long faithfulness possible, and that grace is found in Jesus being the Great High Priest.

That we need a high priest does not immediately resonate with many of us. Before we can turn to discussing *why* we need Jesus to be our Great High Priest (4:14–16; 5:5–10), let's look first at the middle section (5:1–4), at what a high priest did in the covenant God made with Moses.

A HIGH PRIEST

Ordinary priests are one notch below the high priest, and it's a big notch. The term *priest* (Hebrew, *cohen*) occurs over 130 times in the book of Leviticus, and the high priest model for Leviticus was Aaron, the brother of Moses. In today's reading, that priesthood is compared with the priesthood of Jesus. We learn the following five items about the priesthood: First, a priest is appointed by God (Hebrews 5:1, 4). One did not run for priesthood. It was a divinely appointed and then inherited role. By the time of the New Testament, the high priesthood had become far too often a political position engaged in negotiating with Rome, but New Testament–era priests are not the point of our passage. Second, a priest and high priest ultimately came from "among the people," though this means they are humans and not a divine Son of God as Jesus is (5:1; cf. 5:5, 8). Third, a high priest has a ministry *for the people.* The NIV has "to represent the people in matters related to God" (5:1). The addition of "to represent" is implied in the text, which emphasizes their calling for the people. Fourth, their ministry occurs in the temple at the altar in providing for the forgiveness of sins (5:1).

Ministerial roles in the church today need to hear the following words. The fifth feature is noticeably emphasized: They are called to an empathic ministry *because they, like the people, also need the graces of forgiveness* (5:2–4). When the high priest entered into the temple/tabernacle on the Day of Atonement, he first offered sacrifice for his own sins and then for others (Leviticus 16:6 and then 16:15–16). The temple was thus purified for the presence of God. His need for God's grace and forgiveness was to lead him to empathize with the people, expressed in one of the most important pastoral expressions in the Bible: So he is "able to deal gently with those who are ignorant and are going astray" (Hebrews 5:2–3). The term *deal gently* suggests "to moderate passions" (*Second Testament*), especially anger. That is, the empathizing priest (and he empathizes because he, too, is a sinner) is able to "moderate his frustration" (Peeler, *Hebrews*, 146). Jesus, it should be observed, "co-suffers" or sympathizes with our sinfulness; he feels with us but not because he is a sinner. The high priest moderates his own feelings because he is a sinner (4:15; 5:2). The high priest—that is, the Aaron type of priest—needs self-awareness to carry out his ministry. He is one sinner among sinners. He is not superior to the people. Aaron can be a model for some important dimensions of pastoral care in our churches today, and that care can be performed by parents, friends, lay folks, and leaders.

THE GREAT HIGH PRIEST

So why do we need a high priest, and even more, the Great High Priest? Because the goal is the final Rest, and a long faithfulness is the requirement to enter the Rest, and because we cannot get there by our resources, we need help—that is, we need a priest. We need more than help. We are sinners in need of final purification, even perfection, that alone comes from the One who has been perfected. If we sinned in the past, received forgiveness, and then sinned no more, the high priest could remove our sins. But since we continue to sin, and are warned of apostasy, we need the purity empowerments of our Great High Priest who has both pioneered the path for us and continues to mediate on our behalf. David deSilva reminds us once again of the grace that is available to those who turn in faith to God's throne:

The preacher reminds the members of the congregation that they were not left on their own to grit their teeth and push forward. They had open access to the God who would supply them with whatever resources they needed to persevere in the face of hostility and hardship, whether the inner resources of spiritual strength, assurance, and comfort, or the external resources of material aid, loving care and encouragement from their fellow believers in response to God's mobilization of God's own gifts. (deSilva, *Hebrews*, 54)

So, we need the Great High Priest, and that means it's time for us to offer a comprehensive sketch of Jesus as the Great High Priest:*

1. *Appointment:* He is appointed to be the Great High Priest [=GHP] by God (5:5, 10; 7:20–22).
2. *Identification:* He identified with humans in all respects, to the point of suffering (2:9, 11–18; 13:11–14). Hebrews 5:7 alludes to Gethsemane (Matthew 26:38–46; also John 12:27).
3. *Exception:* His identification with us has the important exception: He was totally obedient and sinless (1:9; 4:15; 5:7–10; 7:26–28), and his obedience enabled him to reach the maturation of perfection (5:9). Perfection describes Jesus' total obedience leading to the Father's final approval.
4. *Associations:* His GHP is connected to his apostleship (3:1), his pioneering work (2:10; 12:2), and his sonship (3:5–6; 5:5–6, 8; 10:29).
5. *Benefits:* As GHP he provides access to God for

---

* The word "high" translates *arch* in *archiereus*. The term suggests more senior and seniority than height. Thus, in the *Second Testament* I translate "Senior Priest" (4:14).

strength so we can endure in a long faithfulness (2:1–4, 17–18; 3:14; 4:4–6; 10:19–39; 12:2–3). Because his GHP was confirmed by God with an oath (7:20–22), his GHP is unlike the earthly, Aaron-like high priesthood, which was earthly (9:1–10, 13), imperfect (8:18–19; 10:1–4), and ineffective (8:18; 10:11–14; 13:9–10). Jesus' GHP is a ministry of ultimate salvation (Rest) rendered for humans in heaven (4:14; 5:19–20; 8:1–6; 9:11–28; 12:22–24) and rooted, not in Aaron but in Melchizedek (5:6, 10; 6:13–20; 7:1–28), and is eternal (5:6; 6:20; 7:3, 16–17, 21, 23–25; 13:8), perfect (5:9; 7:11–19, 25, 26–28), and better (7:22; 8:6–13). He intercedes for us (7:25; cf. also Romans 8:34).

6. *Foundations:* His GHP is established by a once-for-all sacrifice of himself (Hebrews 7:27–28; 9:12, 26, 28; 10:5–14) on the basis of a better covenant (8:1–13; 9:11–28; 10:1–18).

7. *Covenant consequences:* Therefore, the Instructor says, the old covenant is fulfilled and terminated in Christ (7:18–19; 8:13).

If the ultimate goal is the Rest, then the need is the One who can get us there. Jesus is that person for the Instructor: He is God's Son, the Apostle of apostles, the Pioneer, and the Great High Priest of all priests and high priests. Even more, he is "the one *who offers,* but also the one *who is offered*" (Brueggemann, *Collected Sermons,* 352), and through those two offerings he makes a way for us. We cannot get to the Rest on our own or in our own powers. We need the One who has perfected the path. As Eugene Peterson once pictured our need for nourishment, "Christian growth, like any kind of growth, needs to be in continuous touch with the sources of its nourishment. If it develops more activity than its roots can support, it loses productivity. If it initiates activity that has no basis in its roots, it will wither quickly, to be replaced the next week by another cut-flower fad" (Peterson, *On Living Well*, 112).

OUR CHALLENGE

We have concentrated our attention on the priestly themes of today's reading, but we can now turn to the discipleship theme. Once again, the theme is a long faithfulness. Another word Hebrews uses for this challenge is *perfection* (2:10; 5:9, 14; 7:19, 28; 9:9; 10:1, 14; 11:40; 12:23). That word can disturb us. I stand with Kathleen Norris when it comes to this term:

> Perfectionism is one of the scariest words I know. . . . The good news about the word "perfect" as used in the New Testament is that it is not a scary word, so much as a scary translation. The word that has been translated as "perfect" does not mean to set forth an impossible goal, or the perfectionism that would have me strive for it at any cost. It is taken from a Latin word meaning complete, entire, full-grown. To those who originally heard it, the word would convey "mature" rather than what we mean today by "perfect." (Norris, *Amazing Grace*, 55, 56)

She then adds this important note: "Perfection, in a Christian sense, means becoming mature enough to give ourself to others. . . . This sort of perfection demands that we become fully ourselves as God would have us: mature, ripe, full, ready for what befalls us, for whatever is to come" (57). In using the term *mature*, Norris strikes the right balance that we express as "long faithfulness" (see sidebar: "Perfection in Hebrews," pp. 83–85).

Two lines jump up to remind us of our calling. In 4:14 we read, "Let us hold firmly to the faith we profess." *Hold firmly* has the sense of grasping and even grabbing onto our confession, which throughout the New Testament has the sense of an open, public agreement that we are followers of Jesus, who himself before Pilate made a similar public confession (2 Corinthians 9:13; 1 Timothy 6:12–13; Hebrews 3:1; 10:23). We should then avoid thinking that our private beliefs or even Sunday morning creedal confessions cover what the Instructor has in mind. Beliefs and creeds are only one part of it; taking a stand with our life covers the whole of it.

Because the goal is the Rest, and because we are sinners in need of empowerment to walk the path of a long faithfulness, we are exhorted to "approach God's throne of grace with confidence" (4:16). Approaching is an important theme for the Instructor (cf. 7:25; 10:1, 22; 11:6; 12:18, 22). The term behind *confidence* (*parrēsia*) has a sense of frankness. That is, we are to approach God and ask God for exactly what we need. God is waiting; God hears us; God wants to empower us. So, let's ask. Here is a beautiful example of approaching God with confidence and frankness:

"Sovereign Lord," they said, "you made the heavens and the earth and the sea, and everything in them. You spoke by the Holy Spirit through the mouth of your servant, our father David:

"'Why do the nations rage and the peoples
plot in vain?
The kings of the earth rise up and the
rulers band together
against the Lord
and against his anointed one.' [from Psalm 2:1–2]

Indeed Herod and Pontius Pilate met together with the Gentiles and the people of Israel in this city to conspire against your holy servant Jesus, whom you anointed. They did what your power and will had decided beforehand should happen. Now, Lord, consider their threats and enable your servants to speak your word with great boldness. Stretch out your hand to heal and perform signs and wonders through the name of your holy servant Jesus."

After they prayed, the place where they were meeting was shaken. And they were all filled with the Holy Spirit and spoke the word of God boldly. (Acts 4:24–31)

In the history of how the church has learned to pray, especially in Sunday worship, these three elements of petitionary prayers are called *invocation, acknowledgment,* and *petition.* Most of our prayers then finish such petitions with an expression of the goal of God's answering the prayer (e.g., "that we may perfectly love") and some expression of the grace foundation for all petitions ("through Christ our Lord" or "in Jesus' name"). Such a form for praying, made eloquently succinct over the years in church "collects" (McKnight, *To You All Hearts Are Open*), arises especially from Old Testament prayers like Deuteronomy 3:23–25; 9:26–29; and 1 Kings 8 (Solomon's long petition). Jesus prayed like this too (Matthew 6:9–13; 11:25–26; John 11:41–42; 12:27–28; 17:1–25), as did the early church (Acts 1:24–25). These "collects" teach us not only how to pray but they teach us how to pray boldly, confidently, and frankly.

Let us then close with this: The challenge is to approach God, but we are to approach God "so that we may receive mercy," that is, forgiveness, "and find grace," because we need God's empowerment, "to help us in our time of need" or "good-timed help" (*Second Testament*), and what we need is the power to live a life of long faithfulness. At the end of today's reading, that long faithfulness is encapsulated in one word: *obey* (5:9).

QUESTIONS FOR REFLECTION AND APPLICATION

1. What do we learn about the ancient Israelite priesthood from this passage?

2. How does Jesus compare and contrast with an Aaronic priest?

3. When do you think Jesus began his high priestly ministry for us? Was it during his life or only after his resurrection and ascension?

4. In what areas of your life do you want Jesus to continue to lead and transform you, so that you can become "perfect," or mature?

5. As you approach God's throne in confidence through prayer today, what do you want to ask God for in order to receive particular mercy and grace?

FOR FURTHER READING

Walter Brueggemann, *The Collected Sermons of Walter Brueggemann* (Philadelphia: Westminster John Knox, 2011).

Scot McKnight, *To You All Hearts Are Open: Revitalizing the Church's Pattern of Asking God* (Brewster, Massachusetts: Paraclete, 2021).

Kathleen Norris, *Amazing Grace: A Vocabulary of Faith* (New York: Riverhead, 1998).

Eugene Peterson, *On Living Well: Brief Reflections on Wisdom for Walking in the Way of Jesus* (Colorado Springs: WaterBrook, 2021).

AN EXHORTATION TO LONG FAITHFULNESS #3

Hebrews 5:11–6:12

[11] We have much to say about this, but it is hard to make it clear to you because you no longer try to understand. [12] In fact, though by this time you ought to be teachers, you need someone to teach you the elementary truths of God's word all over again. You need milk, not solid food! [13] Anyone who lives on milk, being still an infant, is not acquainted with the teaching about righteousness. [14] But solid food is for the mature, who by constant use have trained themselves to distinguish good from evil.

[6:1] Therefore let us move beyond the elementary teachings about Christ and be taken forward to maturity, not laying again the foundation of repentance from acts that lead to death, and of faith in God, [2] instruction about cleansing rites,

the laying on of hands, the resurrection of the dead, and eternal judgment. [3] And God permitting, we will do so.

[4] It is impossible for those who have once been enlightened, who have tasted the heavenly gift, who have shared in the Holy Spirit, [5] who have tasted the goodness of the word of God and the powers of the coming age [6] and who have fallen away, to be brought back to

repentance. To their loss they are crucifying the Son of God all over again and subjecting him to public disgrace. ⁷ Land that drinks in the rain often falling on it and that produces a crop useful to those for whom it is farmed receives the blessing of God. ⁸ But land that produces thorns and thistles is worthless and is in danger of being cursed. In the end it will be burned.

⁹ Even though we speak like this, dear friends, we are convinced of better things in your case—the things that have to do with salvation. ¹⁰ God is not unjust; he will not forget your work and the love you have shown him as you have helped his people and continue to help them. ¹¹ We want each of you to show this same diligence to the very end, so that what you hope for may be fully realized. ¹² We do not want you to become lazy, but to imitate those who through faith and patience inherit what has been promised.

We all sometimes need to be warned. The first warning passage (2:1–4) was brief and fit snugly between two passages comparing Jesus and the angels. The second warning passage, which was a long one, followed a short passage comparing Moses and Jesus (3:1–6 and 3:7–4:13). Today's warning passage follows a fairly short passage comparing Jesus and high priests (4:14–5:10 and 5:11–6:12). The Sermon of Hebrews alternates between (1) comparing Jesus to other notable features in the Bible and (2) warning passages (see Appendix for the book of Hebrews without the warning passages). The audience's spiritual and moral condition greatly concerns the Instructor. He can't move very far into his Sermon without pausing to exhort them to a long faithfulness. His back-and-forth-ness reveals his pastoral touch for those in his care.

A major set of verses, found in the longer warning passage (3:7–4:13), brought to the fore Psalm 95's severe warning. The Instructor is not weaponizing Psalm 95 when he exhorts his audience to recognize they are experiencing a new form of "Today." Nor is he attempting to scare them into obedience and frighten them away from disobedience. The Instructor is a loving pastor exhorting people in his Sermon to choose the path of a long faithfulness. The five warning passages (2:1–4; 3:7–4:13; 5:11–6:12; 10:19–39; 12:4–29), however, strike us all as stiffer challenges than we normally face in our churches. Some today are turned off to Hebrews because of them. The stiffer nature of these warnings reveals the Instructor's situation as distinct. He has turned his pastoral care, which in today's reading shows signs of frustration, toward some believers who are on the verge of turning away from the long faithfulness. As we noted earlier (p. 47), there are four elements in each of these five warning passages: He sketches the audience, he indicates their particular sin, he exhorts them to long faithfulness, and he warns them of the consequences of choosing that particular sin. Today's reflection on the third warning passage clarifies the particular sin.

The warning in the heart of today's passage has acquired the attention of many Bible readers. For many, it is *the* apostasy passage; for others it is a *passage to be explained*; some respond to these others with a snarky "explained *away*"; and for some it is a passage to be *ignored*. It is easy to get lost in a debate about whether or not someone can lose their salvation, but we should observe that salvation in this Sermon does not (fully) occur until the future (cf. 1:14; 6:9; 9:28). In examining if someone can lose what they don't already have (at least entirely), one can entirely miss the heart of the Instructor and his message. In fact, many attempt to bend this passage toward what they want it to say. David deSilva offers this bit of wisdom about reading these verses well: "This is perhaps the most disputed passage in Hebrews, largely because it is often approached from the standpoint of the interpreter's theological convictions and not from the standpoint of the preacher's and his audience's cultural values" (deSilva, *Hebrews*, 61–62). So, let's begin with how he reveals himself and his care in this passage.

THEIR PRESENT AND FUTURE PATH

Our Instructor sounds frustrated with some in his audience. Some would say he's irritated with them. He mentions in passing that he has much more to say, some of which is hard to understand, about Jesus as the Great High Priest, but they "no longer try to understand" (5:11). A literal translation is they have "become sluggish in hearings" (*Second Testament*). Sluggishness is their spiritual condition. He perceives apathy, lethargy, indifference, unresponsiveness, and dullness. Over lunch with a few professor friends, one of them mentioned his undergraduates and said, "I come prepared to teach some students who don't care." Instructors know their experience of enthusiasm for the day's subject that then gets stiff-armed by bored students. When the subject matter is salvation, and the audience is sluggish, we cannot be surprised by an Instructor who turns to warning.

So frustrated is the Instructor that he chastises them for the level of their spiritual formation. They "ought to be teachers" but instead they still "need someone to teach" them (5:12). Some today are in the same phase of spiritual stupor. Instead of teaching Sunday school, or leading a youth group or a Bible study, or sitting on a board at church, they stagnate in a condition that does not exercise the gifts God has given them. As a result, some need to hear "the elementary truths of God's Word all over again"! Their need is the infant's diet instead of the adult's (5:12–13). A mature Christian's diet is "firm provision" (*Second Testament*), which is not about reading thick theology books. Rather, it's about exercising one's spiritual gift. Experienced believers mature by practicing what is "beautiful" and turning away from what is "bad" (5:14; *Second Testament*).* The image, if it were not about such a serious subject, would be laughable: an adult drinking from a baby's milk bottle.

However, frustration is not the Instructor's only mode in today's passage. Jump down to 6:9–10 now. Here we see a tender pastoral encouragement that proceeds positively and affirmatively. "Even though we speak like this" rephrases the warnings from 5:11 through 6:8, and is followed with "dear friends" or, as in *The Second Testament*, "loved ones" (6:9). The Instructor is "persuaded . . . of better things and coming deliverance" for his people (6:9). One could be a touch cynical and say he's entered into the language of psychological motivation with them, but this Sermon is too serious to be manipulative. He really does think they will choose the path of a long faithfulness. One more time, let's remind ourselves: This is about God and God's love and God's grace and God's omniscience. God is both just and will never "forget" how they have walked on the path with Jesus (6:10). They may be not as far along as they ought to be, but they know the path. David deSilva's own pastoral skill comes into play when he fills in some details from this letter about the Instructor's pastoral skills: "Since the preacher will go on shortly to share this 'long and difficult' teaching [5:11] about Jesus anyway (7:1–10:18), and since he does entrust them with one another's perseverance throughout the sermon [e.g., 10:23–25], he clearly believes them up to the task" (deSilva, *Hebrews*, 59).

The Instructor can be frustrated and irritated with his people, but deep down he knows they are believers who will get back on the path of obedience. Or perhaps they have not

---

* The Greek is poetic: *kalos* vs. *kakos*, beautiful vs. bad.

yet left it but have decided to stop. Perhaps then they just need to take new first steps along the path. He's confident they will go forward in the faith. His pastoral words here, like those in 10:39, 12:22, and 28–29, require us then to think of the audience not only as believers but as believers who will rise to the challenge of long faithfulness.

THEIR PAST COMMITMENTS

For many of us, then, the list of the audience's past commitments reveals that they are genuine, if wobbly, believers. We discussed the audience as believers at 3:1–19 in the section "The Audience" (see pp. 48–49). In Hebrews 6:1–3 we learn about six features of these elementary teachings they had embraced. These are foundations for them, echoing 5:12–14, to move on to "maturity" (6:1) or toward "completeness" (*Second Testament*), and often translated "perfection" (NRSVue). In this Everyday Bible Study, the term *perfection* is encapsulated in *long faithfulness*. The foundation of all spiritual formation is "conversion" (*Second Testament*) or, as in the NIV, "repentance from acts that lead to death" (6:1).

Upon this foundation the Instructor reminds his people of five features of that foundation: (1) "faith in God," (2) "instruction about cleansing rites," which indicates a Jewish heritage, (3) "the laying on of hands," which indicates the invocation and reception of the Spirit, (4) "the resurrection of the dead," which was the bedrock truth of the gospel, and (5) "eternal judgment," which no one who has read Hebrews this far can have missed. If the Rest is the ultimate goal of long faithfulness, the final judgment is the next-to-last step—the last being endless dancing and walking in the kingdom. Those who enter the kingdom have reached "perfection," which as I have just noted, can be summed up in having achieved "long faithfulness."

Let's pause then for a brief discussion of perfection in Hebrews. Jesus himself, it must be noted, was made perfect by his obedience in the midst of suffering (2:10; 5:9; 7:28; 10:14). This sets the whole tone for the meaning of perfection: It is an affirmative divine evaluation at the end of life for having accomplished God's will for that person. Perfection does not refer to sinlessness. As the one and only who was made perfect, Jesus can accomplish salvation for all of us (5:9; 12:2). Neither the law nor the Levitical system can accomplish that kind of perfection (7:11, 19; 9:9; 10:1; 11:40). Because of God's redemptive empowerment in us through the Spirit, a redemptive empowerment that is better and perfect (9:11; 12:2, 23), we are called to perfection (6:1; cf. 11:40). In sum, perfection refers to God's final stamp of approval of a life of long faithfulness. We are in the age of being perfected, Christ is the Perfect One and the Perfector of our faith in his ministry of intercession, and we are called to perfection (a life of obedience).

The pastoral care of the Instructor knows that last element, eternal judgment, needs attention for his audience. They have the capacity and evidently the possibility of committing a sin with grave consequences, and we now want to clarify what that sin is.

Perfection in Hebrews

(emphasis added)

Heb. 2:10 *In bringing many sons and daughters to glory, it was fitting that God, for whom and through whom everything exists, should make the pioneer of their salvation **perfect** through what he suffered.*

Heb. 5:9 . . . *and, once made **perfect**, he became the source of eternal salvation for all who obey him . . .*

Heb. 6:1 *Therefore let us move beyond the elementary teachings about Christ and be taken forward to maturity [**perfection**], not laying again the foundation of repentance from acts that lead to death, and of faith in God . . .*

Heb. 7:11 *If **perfection** could have been attained through the Levitical priesthood—and indeed the law given to the people established that priesthood—why was there still need for another priest to come, one in the order of Melchizedek, not in the order of Aaron?*

Heb. 7:19 . . . *(for the law made nothing **perfect**), and a better hope is introduced, by which we draw near to God.*

Heb. 7:28 *For the law appoints as high priests men in all their weakness; but the oath, which came after the law, appointed the Son, who has been made **perfect** forever.*

Heb. 9:9 *This is an illustration for the present time, indicating that the gifts and sacrifices being offered were not able to clear [**perfect**] the conscience of the worshiper.*

Heb. 9:11 *But when Christ came as high priest of the good things that are now already here, he went through the greater and more **perfect** tabernacle that is not made with human hands, that is to say, is not a part of this creation.*

Heb. 10:1 *The law is only a shadow of the good things that are coming—not the realities themselves. For this reason it can never, by the same sacrifices repeated endlessly year after year, make* **perfect** *those who draw near to worship.*

Heb. 10:14 *For by one sacrifice he has made* **perfect** *forever those who are being made holy.*

Heb. 11:40 . . . *since God had planned something better for us so that only together with us would they be made* **perfect***.*

Heb. 12:2 . . . *fixing our eyes on Jesus, the pioneer and* **perfecter** *of faith. For the joy set before him he endured the cross, scorning its shame, and sat down at the right hand of the throne of God.*

Heb. 12:23 . . . *to the church of the firstborn, whose names are written in heaven. You have come to God, the Judge of all, to the spirits of the righteous made* **perfect** . . .

THE PRESENT WARNING

At 6:4–6 he clarifies again that they are believers, speaking of his audience as those who know the greatness of God's amazing grace. They (1) "have once been enlightened," (2) "have tasted the heavenly gift," (3) "have shared in the Holy Spirit," (4) "have tasted the goodness of the word of God" and (5) "the powers of the coming age" (6:4–5). These are all early Christian terms for those who have experienced God's grace, conversion, regeneration, and new life.

Even with the terms in the previous paragraph as clear, the Instructor flat-out warns people who have been catechized (6:1–3) and converted (6:4–5) that, if they commit the sin of falling off the path (6:6), it will be "impossible" (NIV) or they will find themselves "powerless" (*Second Testament*) to get back on the path (6:4). I like how Amy Peeler fastens onto the sense of these verses: "An initial confession still demands a perpetual faith. An initial repentance still demands a continual rejection of sin. These are both one-time events and continual realities" (Peeler, *Hebrews*, 162). Second repentances leading to second conversions are impossible. Hearts that move into sluggishness and dullness are early indicators of the possibility of moving into more serious conditions of spiritual torpor, apostasy, and death. Hearts that have been awakened and then die don't reawaken. Well-watered fields produce edible fruits; lands producing "thorns and thistles" indicate their lack of life and solid nutrients (6:7–8). The problem here is not God's. The problem is that the human has chosen a way of heart and life that makes that person unwilling, even unable, to cross the Jordan into the promised land.

Apostasy in Hebrews

Although there is great danger involved in any sinning, apostasy is most devastatingly dangerous. The tragedy of apostasy is that one deliberately steps aside from the truth, with a full change of mind about it all, and with an offensive attitude toward what one once embraced as worthy of trust. Only someone who has once believed can be guilty of such a sin, which shows the spirit of rejection where faith once motivated them.

> . . . Devotion and diligence demand each other, and they indelibly mark the true disciple of the Lord.
>
> From James Earl Massey and Jennifer T. Kaalund, "Hebrews," 479.

We ask, *What is the sin about which the Instructor is so concerned?* Hebrews 6:6 labels it "falling away" or "falling off the path." Our method, as we made clear when we discussed the audience at 3:7–4:13, is to synthesize the terms in all five warning passages. So, we need to look at how the Instructor describes this Sin in those passages. Not tabulating duplicates, there are about forty different terms used in this Sermon. Some words are so metaphorical it's hard to put clarity on them, like "slip away" (2:1) or "sluggish" (5:11; 6:12). Let's turn to the more explicit and distinct terms. I italicize the specifics:

> See to it, brothers and sisters, that none of you has a sinful, unbelieving heart that *turns away from the living God*. (3:12)

> . . . and who have *fallen away*, to be brought back to repentance. To their loss they are *crucifying the Son of God all over again and subjecting him to public disgrace*. (6:6)

> If we *deliberately keep on sinning* after we have received the knowledge of the truth, no sacrifice for sins is left. (10:26)

> How much more severely do you think someone deserves to be punished who has *trampled the Son of*

God underfoot, who has *treated as an unholy thing the blood of the covenant that sanctified them,* and who has *insulted the Spirit of grace?* (10:29)

See to it that you do not *refuse him who speaks.* If they did not escape when they refused him who warned them on earth, how much less will we, if we *turn away from him who warns us from heaven?* (12:25)

Hebrews 3:12 uses a term (*apostēnai*) from which we get the term *apostasy*. That term is clarified further with falling away from Jesus Christ, the crucified one, and the message of the cross (6:6). The sin the Instructor has in mind is one that does not sneak up on someone, and neither is it a sin about which they are unaware. No, it is a deliberate and therefore conscious act of turning one's back on Jesus (10:26). Furthermore, even those who have been "sanctified" have the capacity and possibility of turning against Jesus Christ and treat the blood of Jesus as a common, unholy item (10:29). Topping that action is insulting the Spirit of God (10:29). Finally, the sin involves refusing to heed what they hear from God (12:25).

Now defined, the particular sin for this particular audience was willful rejection of God, his Son, Jesus Christ, and the Holy Spirit in an open, conscious denunciation. This sin then is deliberate and conscious; it is Trinitarian; and it is behavioral (or moral). This is the sin of Christian apostasy. Those who have committed apostasy not only know so, but they take delight and hubris in their decision. Those who worry over whether they have or have not committed this sin are not to worry. Apostates don't worry; they know what they have done. Amy Peeler clarifies the sense of the exhortations: "If someone is heartbroken that they may have fallen away from the faith, that concern over one's relationship with God is evidence that they have *not* fallen away" (Peeler, *Hebrews*, 164).

The pastoral heart of the Instructor grieves over this possibility, but as we saw above, he is confident his audience will choose to take the next steps on the path of long faithfulness. His confidence is rooted in God's goodness (6:10), not in their morality. So, he exhorts them with these words: "We want each of you to show this same diligence to the very end, so that what you hope for may be fully realized. We do not want you to become lazy, but to imitate those who through faith and patience inherit what has been promised" (6:11–12). Such words imply the genuine possibility and capacity of the audience to make the good choice.

The exhortations and warnings of Hebrews are designed to grab our attention and to press us into self-inspection. They make me wonder how I'm doing with God, but more than that, they urge me to be more resilient, more dedicated, and more devoted to following Jesus. Each of us, in reading these warnings, asks, *What can I do today so what happened to the apostates does not happen to me?* A pastor friend of mine recently told me his pattern has been to "talk with God" in the morning by spending time with the Word, and to "talk with humans" in the afternoon. His life permits his mornings to be spent in communion with God, and it shows in his personal walk with Christ. Most of us don't have that privilege. But what we can do is carve out time each day for quiet attentiveness to the words of the Bible and to conversation with God. Over time, such a practice will stimulate our feet into walking more vigorously and confidently on the path of long faithfulness.

QUESTIONS FOR REFLECTION
AND APPLICATION

1. What do you think of the structure of this Sermon, alternating between comparisons about Jesus and warnings?

2. When have you felt frustrated with people you teach or lead who seem sluggish, bored, immature, or not using their gifts?

3. If perfection here does not mean sinlessness, what does it mean in the life of the believer?

4. How would you summarize the meaning of the sin of apostasy according to Hebrews?

5. What practices would you like to cultivate in your life to help you talk with God more?

THE PROMISE
UNDERGIRDING A
LONG FAITHFULNESS

Hebrews 6:13–20

[13] When God made his promise to Abraham, since there was no one greater for him to swear by, he swore by himself, [14] saying, "I will surely bless you and give you many descendants." [15] And so after waiting patiently, Abraham received what was promised.

[16] People swear by someone greater than themselves, and the oath confirms what is said and puts an end to all argument. [17] Because God wanted to make the unchanging nature of his purpose very clear to the heirs of what was promised, he confirmed it with an oath. [18] God did this so that, by two unchangeable things in which it is impossible for God to lie, we who have fled to take hold of the hope set before us may be greatly encouraged. [19] We have this hope as an anchor for the soul, firm and secure. It enters the inner sanctuary behind the curtain, [20] where our forerunner, Jesus, has entered on our behalf. He has become a high priest forever, in the order of Melchizedek.

*L*et's talk about God. That's what I hear from the Instructor. He has warned and warned and warned.

He knows what happens in the heart of believers who hear too much warning. They get anxious and worried about both their self-perception *(Am I a genuine believer?)*, their security *(Have I committed apostasy?)*, and their future destiny *(Will I in the final day be banished?)*. So, true pastor that he is, the Instructor backs off, shifts registers, and decides to talk about the utter security of God's promise. After all, he has just stated he is "convinced of better things" about them (6:9–12). Undergirding his confidence and their faithfulness is a God who has entered into a covenantal promise to which God is faithful. The long faithfulness of believers is only possible because of the long faithfulness of God, and God's patience calls us to imitate Abraham's patience (6:12, 15).

We have a tendency to fall asleep on God and to seek contentment in ourselves—what we can do, what we know, what we accomplish. Long faithfulness awakens to God, and it sees God everywhere in such a way that life becomes the pilgrimage God intended. I like how Barbara Brown Taylor speaks of altars in this world. She once wrote, "Human beings may separate things into as many piles as we wish— separating spirit from flesh, sacred from secular, church from world. But we should not be surprised when God does not recognize the distinctions we make between the two. Earth is so thick with divine possibility that it is a wonder we can walk anywhere without cracking our shins on altars" (Taylor, *Altar*, 15). I like that because I know I can fall asleep and fail to recognize God all around me.

Let's reframe this for ourselves: The ultimate goal is the Rest, which is the promise of eternally dwelling in the innermost presence of God. I am at times asked if I believe in heaven and why I believe in heaven. My reason is this: God has promised, and what God has promised has been proven to come true. God cannot undo his commitment to perfect us and all creation. This is the logic at work in today's passage. What undergirds our long faithfulness is "the certainty of God's Word" (Pierce, "Hebrews," 593).

A Promise to Abraham

God entered into a covenant with Abram (Genesis 12; 15), and in that covenant God promised that Abram's descendants would become a "great nation" and through him and that nation "all the peoples on earth will be blessed" (12:2–3). In the heart of that promise was that Abram and Sarai would have a son (13:15–17), which some years later created consternation over "no baby" (15:2–3). God interrupts Abram and reaffirms the promise and so enters into a covenant (15:6–20). God changes his name to "Abraham," the father of many nations (17:5), the distinguishing mark of circumcision is given, and, in spite of their impatience and foolishness, their son Isaac is born. Genesis 21:1 reads that God "did for Sarah what he had promised." That child was sealed as the descendant in the famous offering of Isaac that expressed Abraham's faithfulness to the faithful, providing God (Genesis 22). There are then four moments in the Abrahamic promise. They build on one another:

> The promise(s) of Genesis 12,
> the covenant engagement of Genesis 15,
> the rite of circumcision in Genesis 17,
> and the sealing of faithfulness of the near offering of
> Isaac in Genesis 22.

To speak of the latter is to speak of other three. Hebrews sees all four through the lens of Genesis 22. Each of these chapters were altars for Abraham and can be for us as we seek the promise God has made.

The Instructor provides insight into the promise and covenant: "Since there was no one greater for him to swear by, he swore by himself" that an abundance of descendants would establish his line (Hebrews 6:13, 14; citing Genesis 22:17). This singularity of God as the Actor in the promissory covenant (Genesis 15; 22) turns all the attention away from humans and toward God. The Instructor's logic is obvious: *If God was faithful to that promise, he will be faithful to the promise to those in the line of Christ.* This God, he is saying to his people, alone is the Great God.

A Promise Secured by an Oath

I cracked my shin on the altar of his insight that comes next. The promise, which became a covenant promise, was established by an "oath," which "puts an end to all argument" (Hebrews 6:16, referring to the oath of Genesis 22:17). God's promise takes on the characteristic of "unchangeableness" (6:17; *Second Testament*) because God has entered into a double promise: both the covenant promise and oath with Abraham, and the covenant promise and oath with Jesus (7:21; 8:7–13), neither of which can change because both are secured by a legal, covenantal arrangement (6:18). On oath, perhaps you will find these words as helpful as I find them: "God used an oath because of the oath's significance in human society. An oath was the ultimate way for a person to affirm his integrity. When one swore an oath one called on 'someone greater' (God) to attest one's faithfulness and to punish one's unfaithfulness with death. The ancients took oaths very seriously. There was no greater way to convince others of one's honesty and faithfulness" (Cockerill, *Hebrews*, 55). If God pledges doubly to secure the promise, the ultimate fulfillment of which is the Rest, then we can be assured of entering into the Rest.

God's Oaths/Swearing

Luke 1:73 . . . *the oath he swore to our father Abraham . . .*

Acts 2:30 *But he was a prophet and knew that God had promised him on oath that he would place one of his descendants on his throne.*

Heb. 3:11 *So I declared on oath in my anger,*
"They shall never enter my rest."

Heb. 3:18 *And to whom did God swear that they would never enter his rest if not to those who disobeyed?*

Heb. 4:3 *Now we who have believed enter that rest, just as God has said,*

"So I declared on oath in my anger,
'They shall never enter my rest.'"

And yet his works have been finished since the creation of the world.

Heb. 6:13 *When God made his promise to Abraham, since there was no one greater for him to swear by, he swore by himself. . .*

Heb 6:17 *Because God wanted to make the unchanging nature of his purpose very clear to the heirs of what was promised, he confirmed it with an oath.*

Heb 7:20–21 *And it was not without an oath! Others*

became priests without any oath, [21] but he became a priest with an oath when God said to him:

"The Lord has sworn
    and will not change his mind:
        'You are a priest forever.'"

Heb 7:28 *For the law appoints as high priests men in all their weakness; but the oath, which came after the law, appointed the Son, who has been made perfect forever.*

A PROMISE TO US

The Instructor shifts from the "you" of the warnings to a "we" of the covenant promise (6:18–20), thus including himself into the grand expansiveness of God's promise to the whole people of God. The "we" are those who "have fled to take hold of the hope" (6:18) and who have this "hope as an anchor for the soul, firm and secure" (6:19). Hope curbs our steps onto the path and toward the Rest. As Frederck Buechner reminds us, "For Christians, hope is ultimately hope in Christ. The hope that he really is what for centuries we have been claiming he is. The hope that despite the fact that sin and death still rule the world, he somehow conquered them. The hope that in him and through him all of us stand a chance of somehow conquering them too. The hope that at some unforeseeable time and in some unimaginable way he will return with healing in his wings" (Buechner, *Beyond Words*, 160).

To which location have we fled? Here the Instructor begins a shift to a brand-new theological topic, making it clear that we have fled to "the inner sanctuary behind the curtain," that is, the holy of holies, that is, to the very intense presence of God. In the holiest of sacred spaces one finds Jesus, who as the Pioneer (2:10; 12:2) is now the Forerunner, and as the Great High Priest has finally accomplished a better, perfect redemption (6:20). "Jesus's representative entering in has at least two dimensions. First, as the representative human who reigns (2:7–8), he shows other humans that such entrance, and the reigning that comes with it, is possible. Second, as the advocating human who represents us to the Father (4:14–15), his entrance aids the humans who were following him as they journey to his location" (Peeler, *Hebrews*, 180).

The Instructor closes down our chapter six with a name that will soon occupy his, and therefore our, attention. Jesus' priestly order is not that of Aaron but of *Melchizedek*. This connection will shape what we read all the way into chapter ten. We need a mediator, a priest, remember, because the ultimate goal is the Rest, the requirement is a long faithfulness, we cannot do it on our own, and the power does not come from us—but from God, Father, Son, and Spirit. The Aaronic priesthood lacked the capacities to lead us to the perfection of the Rest; the Melchizedekian priesthood provides the order of perfection.

QUESTIONS FOR REFLECTION AND APPLICATION

1. Take some time to read Genesis 12–22, reflecting on what a long faithfulness looked like for Abraham and Sarah. How was their life like and unlike yours?

2. Look up Hebrews 6:17; 8:6; 10:23; 11:11; 12:26. What do you notice about God as one who keeps promises?

3. When have you worried about the state of your soul or the security of your salvation?

4. How does this passage about the security of God's promise encourage you?

5. What "altars" to God's faithfulness have you seen in your life or in Scripture that sustain your hope?

FOR FURTHER READING

Frederick Buechner, *Beyond Words: Daily Readings in the ABC's of Faith* (San Francisco: HarperSanFrancisco, 2004).

Barbara Brown Taylor, *An Altar in the World: A Geography of Faith* (New York: HarperOne, 2009).

THE SON'S LONG FAITHFULNESS AS MELCHIZEDEK

Hebrews 6:19–7:28

[19b] *[Our hope] enters the inner sanctuary behind the curtain,* [20] *where our forerunner, Jesus, has entered on our behalf. He has become a high priest forever, in the order of Melchizedek.*

[7:1] *This Melchizedek was king of Salem and priest of God Most High. He met Abraham returning from the defeat of the kings and blessed him,* [2] *and Abraham gave him a tenth of everything. First, the name Melchizedek means "king of righteousness"; then also, "king of Salem" means "king of peace."* [3] *Without father or mother, without genealogy, without beginning of days or end of life, resembling the Son of God, he remains a priest forever.*

[4] *Just think how great he was: Even the patriarch Abraham gave him a tenth of the plunder!* [5] *Now the law requires the descendants of Levi who become priests to collect a tenth from the people—that is, from their fellow Israelites—even though they also are descended from Abraham.* [6] *This man, however, did not trace his descent from Levi, yet he collected a tenth from Abraham and blessed him who had the promises.* [7] *And without doubt the lesser is blessed by the greater.* [8] *In the one case, the tenth is collected by people who die; but*

in the other case, by him who is declared to be living. ⁹ One might even say that Levi, who collects the tenth, paid the tenth through Abraham, ¹⁰ because when Melchizedek met Abraham, Levi was still in the body of his ancestor.

¹¹ If perfection could have been attained through the Levitical priesthood—and indeed the law given to the people established that priesthood—why was there still need for another priest to come, one in the order of Melchizedek, not in the order of Aaron? ¹² For when the priesthood is changed, the law must be changed also. ¹³ He of whom these things are said belonged to a different tribe, and no one from that tribe has ever served at the altar. ¹⁴ For it is clear that our Lord descended from Judah, and in regard to that tribe Moses said nothing about priests. ¹⁵ And what we have said is even more clear if another priest like Melchizedek appears, ¹⁶ one who has become a priest not on the basis of a regulation as to his ancestry but on the basis of the power of an indestructible life.

¹⁷ For it is declared:

> "You are a priest forever,
>   in the order of Melchizedek."

¹⁸ The former regulation is set aside because it was weak and useless ¹⁹ (for the law made nothing perfect), and a better hope is introduced, by which we draw near to God.

²⁰ And it was not without an oath! Others became priests without any oath, ²¹ but he became a priest with an oath when God said to him:

> "The Lord has sworn
>   and will not change his mind:
>   'You are a priest forever.'"

²² Because of this oath, Jesus has become the guarantor of a better covenant.

23 Now there have been many of those priests, since death pre-vented them from continuing in office; 24 but because Jesus lives for-ever, he has a permanent priesthood. 25 Therefore he is able to save completely those who come to God through him, because he always lives to intercede for them.

26 Such a high priest truly meets our need—one who is holy, blameless, pure, set apart from sinners, exalted above the heavens. 27 Unlike the other high priests, he does not need to offer sacrifices day after day, first for his own sins, and then for the sins of the people. He sacrificed for their sins once for all when he offered him-self. 28 For the law appoints as high priests men in all their weakness; but the oath, which came after the law, appointed the Son, who has been made perfect forever.

You may have been even more surprised than the Instructor's first hearers when the last verse of chapter six ended with the notion that Jesus became a high priest forever *in the order of Melchizedek*. In fact, you may have squinted as so many Bible readers have done, wondering your whole face into the question, "Who in the world is Melchizedek?" He is almost as surprising of a figure to nearly all Bible readers as some Bible teacher you know being compared to Nicolaus of Cusa! (I assume you don't know much more than I do about that fifteenth century German theologian.) It's possible the Instructor's readers had heard someone read Genesis 14:7–10 lately, but my guess is that they were quite surprised when Jesus was compared with Melchizedek. Angels, fine; Moses, for sure; the high priests, sure; the covenant, yes; and the law, of course. But Melchizedek? Let's dig into this figure and see what turns up. But before doing that, we need a reminder.

Every time we partake in the Eucharist (or communion or the Lord's Supper or Mass), we enter once again into the holy of holies to participate in the redemptive priesthood of Jesus Christ, our Great High Priest. Some of us partake daily, some weekly, some monthly, and some quarterly. I have my opinion on how often (weekly), but that is not the issue here. All day long, every day, weekly, monthly, and quarterly, Jesus is interceding for us. Today's reading says about Jesus that he is "living always to intercede" for his people (7:25; *Second Testament*). Hebrews expounds, extends, expands, and enlarges the Eucharist. Our Great High Priest, who draws us to the Table to know his grace, his forgiveness, and his redemption, empowers us into his own long faithfulness. Jesus "has made it possible at last for God's people to cross formerly impassable boundaries in their approach to God (that is, entry into God's full presence in the eternal realm)" (deSilva, *Hebrews*, 73–74).

By the way, chapters seven through ten in Hebrews are often described as the most difficult in the book. The Instructor said as much when, in 5:11, he wrote, "We have much to say about this," and he had just mentioned Melchizedek in 5:10, "but it is hard to make it clear to you." So, he was right, and so it remains difficult even for those with open hearts and minds!

MELCHIZEDEK

So you don't have to try to keep your Bible open to two passages, here is what Genesis 14 records about the appearance of Melchizedek to Abram:

> [17] After Abram returned from defeating Kedorlaomer and the kings allied with him, the king of Sodom came out to meet him in the Valley of Shaveh (that is, the King's Valley). [18] Then Melchizedek king of Salem brought out bread and wine. He was priest of God Most High, [19] and he blessed Abram, saying,
>
> "Blessed be Abram by God Most High,
> Creator of heaven and earth.

[20] And praise be to God Most High,
   who delivered your enemies into your hand."

Then Abram gave him a tenth of everything.

The Instructor more or less repeats what he found in Genesis. But his lens changes everything because his lens gives him eyes to see what others had not seen. The Instructor sees Jesus in Melchizedek. After rehearsing the basics in Genesis (Hebrews 7:1–2a), the Instructor unfolds what he sees in this "priest of God Most High." Remember, if the prophet's job was to carry a message from God to the people, in general the priest's job was to carry the people to God. First, he turns to the man's name and title: His name means king of *righteousness* (Hebrew, *zedek*) and his title means king of *peace* (Hebrew, *salem*, from which we get *shalom*).

Then the Instructor fills in the biographical gaps between the lines in Genesis 14. But we need to pause: The Instructor reads Genesis 14 through the lens of Psalm 110:4, where we encounter the famous line that the king of Salem was a priest forever. So, the Old Testament itself filled in the gap before the Instructor did. We do find in the Dead Sea Scrolls more information about Melchizedek, but the Instructor shows no significant awareness of what was said there. Instead, Melchizedek had become a rich source to explore for Bible experts. But because of the gaps and the gap filled in Psalm 110, the Instructor provides details in those gaps. Melchizedek was "without father or mother, without genealogy, without beginning of days or end of life"—and these gap-fillers are supported by the man's absence in the genealogies in Genesis 9–11. *Therefore*, the king of Salem is "comparable to God's Son," and what is comparable is the endlessness of his priesthood (Hebrews 7:3; *Second Testament*). The crucial insight for the Instructor turns on Jesus' priesthood, unlike all the priests and high priests of Israel and its surrounding cities, being eternal. Amy Peeler reframes the entirety of the priesthood connected to Aaron, Levi, and Moses in these breathtaking terms: "The Melchizedekian priesthood of Jesus is not superior because it is brand-new, a replacement for the Levitical. It gives no evidence that God is changing course. Quite the opposite. The author discovers in Genesis 14 that this superior priesthood has existed even before Levi was born. Levi and those in his line were always meant to serve in deference to, by pointing the way to another priesthood" (Peeler, *Hebrews*, 192). This is what is breathtaking: The generations of priests and high priests from Moses on were but manifestations of the priesthood of Melchizedek, and Melchizedek himself anticipated the high priesthood of Jesus.

Once again we are face-to-face with the *long* faithfulness of Jesus, whom we partake of in the elements of the Eucharist. Not only was he faithful as a Son in his earthly days, he remains faithful to his redemptive work throughout all eternity. Because of his long faithfulness, the believers have a Pioneer and an advocate who is the Great High Priest (2:10, 14–18; 4:14–16). When the ultimate goal is the Rest, and when the requirement is a long faithfulness, what a believer most needs is the nourishment and strength to carry on. In Jesus, the Melchizedekian priest, one finds that strength.

Melchizedek poses a problem for those who know Israel's story. The highest ranking individuals in that story are Abraham and Moses. How can the Instructor suggest Melchizedek, who is in the type of Jesus' eternal priesthood, outrank them? The fact is that for the Instructor, he does because he is a priest forever. Notice how he pulls this off in 7:4–10. How is Melchizedek greater than Abraham? Working from the gaps in 7:3 as read through Psalm 110:4, the Instructor works back in time to a period well before the priests. Israelites, eventually, will be required to pay a tithe to the priests in the tabernacle and then in the temple of Jerusalem. Though not in the priestly line of Levi, and well before Levi, Melchizedek collected a tithe from Abraham and then blessed the patriarch. That's fact one. The fundamental blessing-principle the Instructor sees here is that the "lesser" is blessed by the "greater" (7:7). That's fact two. The word behind "greater" (*kreittōn*) can be translated as "better," "greater," and "superior" (see the sidebar: "'Better' Things in Hebrews," pp. 105–107). Now fact three: The better-ness of Melchizedek here is because he is a priest forever, while the other priests die (7:8). He reflects further with fact four: Levi, who descends from Abraham, can be said to have paid tithes in Abraham to Melchizedek (7:9–10).

"Better" Things in Hebrews

(emphasis added)

Heb. 1:4 *So he became as much* superior *to the angels as the name he has inherited is superior to theirs.*

Heb. 6:9 *Even though we speak like this, dear friends, we are convinced of* better *things in your case—the things that have to do with salvation.*

Heb. 7:7 *And without doubt the lesser is blessed by the* greater.

Heb. 7:19 . . . *(for the law made nothing perfect), and a* better *hope is introduced, by which we draw near to God.*

Heb. 7:22 *Because of this oath, Jesus has become the guarantor of a* better *covenant.*

Heb. 8:6 *But in fact the ministry Jesus has received is as* superior *to theirs as the covenant of which he is mediator is* superior *to the old one, since the new covenant is established on better promises.*

Heb. 9:23 *It was necessary, then, for the copies of the heavenly things to be purified with these sacrifices, but the heavenly things themselves with* better *sacrifices than these.*

Heb. 10:34 *You suffered along with those in prison and joyfully accepted the confiscation of your property, because you knew that you yourselves had* better *and lasting possessions.*

Heb. 11:4 *By faith Abel brought God a* better *offering than Cain did. By faith he was commended as righteous, when God spoke well of his offerings. And by faith Abel still speaks, even though he is dead.*

Heb. 11:16 *Instead, they were longing for a* better *country—a heavenly one. Therefore God is not ashamed to be called their God, for he has prepared a city for them.*

Heb. 11:35 *Women received back their dead, raised to life again. There were others who were tortured, refusing to be released so that they might gain an even* better *resurrection.*

Heb. 11:40 . . . *since God had planned something* better *for us so that only together with us would they be made perfect.*

> Heb. 12:24 . . . to *Jesus the mediator of a new covenant,*
> *and to the sprinkled blood that speaks a* better *word*
> *than the blood of Abel.*

JESUS COMPARED WITH MELCHIZEDEK

Anticipating the direct comparisons of Jesus with Melchizedek,* the Instructor informs his listeners that "perfection" was not accomplished "through the Levitical priesthood" (7:11) (see sidebar: "The Meaning of Perfection in Hebrews," pp. 108–109). If the priesthood of Melchizedek is a forever priesthood (5:6; 7:3), and the priesthood in the Levi line is not, then Melchizedek transcends Levi. This reveals that the words about Melchizedek have an eschatological shape: What was said to him were words anticipating their fullness in Christ (7:11–13). Recall the Instructor's thoughts here are based on Genesis 14 as interpreted by Psalm 110:4. In fact, Hebrews 7:15–25 explains Jesus on the basis of Psalm 110:4, which is quoted in Hebrews 7:17 and 21. Because of Psalm 110:4's word "forever," there is "no succession necessary—or possible" (Massey-Kaalund, "Hebrews," 480).

Close readers may have anticipated a problem. *Priests are in the line of Levi; Jesus is not a Levite; he is a Judahite, and Judahites are not priests* (7:14). But the Instructor anticipating this says, the importance of Melchizedek "is even more clear if another priest like Melchizedek appears" (7:15). The basis of his priesthood is not ancestry but eternality (7:16–17), an eternality rooted in God's eternality in faithfulness and Jesus' eternality expressed in his long faithfulness as the

---

* Some have suggested Melchizedek was a "christophany," an actual appearance of Christ. But the text of Hebrews clearly reads as if they are two beings. For a discussion, see Peeler, *Hebrews*, 186–188.

Great High Priest. All of these ideas form a network in Hebrews. We must admit that most of us today do not operate in that network of terms, so reading this letter can be a challenge both to understand and to see the relevance of. The relevance, we insist, is the Son's long faithfulness *for us* and our need to live out a long faithfulness. This is the "better hope" of which the Instructor speaks (7:19).

The Instructor would perhaps have made some enemies with some of his terms about the old priesthood. He says it was "weak and useless" because the law was unable to lead to perfection (7:18–19). Another element of better-ness is the important term "oath," which is found in the opening words of Psalm 110:4: "The Lord has sworn and will not change his mind" (found in Hebrews 7:20–22). Melchizedek's priesthood came with an oath, and this makes Jesus a "guarantor of a better covenant" (7:22). Oath-ness is tied to this guarantor and better covenant, but once again this is all tied to the foreverness of the priestly work of Jesus for us. That is, he constantly intercedes for us (7:23–25). If he is doing that for us, then we can be assured of the perfection of our long faithfulness. The benefit of Jesus' priesthood is that he can "save completely," though this term echoes the idea of perfection, and it could be paraphrased as saving perfectly or delivering us into perfection.

The Meaning of Perfection in Hebrews

Jesus himself was made perfect by his obedience in the midst of suffering (2:10; 5:9; 7:28; 10:14). This sets the whole tone for the meaning of perfection: It is an affirmative divine evaluation at the end of life for having accomplished God's will for that person. As one who was made perfect, he can accomplish salvation for all of us (5:9; 12:2). Neither the law nor the Levitical system can accomplish that kind of·perfection (7:11, 19; 9:9; 10:1; 11:40). Because of God's redemptive empowerment in us through the Spirit, a redemptive empowerment that is better and perfect (9:11; 12:2, 23), we are called to perfection (6:1; cf. 11:40). In sum, perfection refers to God's final stamp of approval of a life of long faithfulness. We are in the age of being perfected, Christ is the Perfect One and the Perfector of our faith in his ministry of intercession, and we are called to perfection (a life of obedience).

His complete redemptive work faces us in the elements of the Eucharist. When we partake of the bread and wine, we are publicly affirming that we find our redemption in Jesus. That we partake in the Lord's supper so often reminds us, too, of his ongoing interceding for us (7:25). One of the Exhortations used in *The Book of Common Prayer* to open what is called "The Holy Eucharist" reads like this:

Beloved in the Lord: Our Savior Christ, on the night before he suffered, instituted the Sacrament of his Body and Blood as a sign and pledge of his love, for the continual remembrance of the sacrifice of his death, and for a spiritual sharing in his risen life. Or in these holy Mysteries we are made one with Christ, and Christ with us; We are made one body in him, and members one of another. (*The Book of Common Prayer*, 316)

Following the words that remind us of the need for obedience, and how we at times fall short, we confess our sins, and in this we echo 1 John 1:9's reminder to confess as we remember, too, that God forgives the confessor. Here are the words of a confession from the same *Book of Common Prayer*:

> Most merciful God, we confess that we have sinned against you in thought, word, and deed, by what we have done, and by what we have left undone. We have not loved you with our whole heart; We have not loved our neighbors as ourselves. We are truly sorry and we humbly repent. For the sake of your son Jesus Christ, have mercy on us and forgive us; that we may delight in your will, and walk in your ways, to the glory of your name. Amen. (*The Book of Common Prayer*, 320, with slight adjustments to modern English)

Following our confession, the pastor or priest in this tradition reminds us of God's long faithfulness in forgiveness by pronouncing words of absolution:

> Almighty God, our heavenly Father, who of his great mercy has promised forgiveness of sins to all those who with hearty repentance and true faith turn unto him, have mercy upon you, pardon and deliver you from all your sins, confirm and strengthen you in all goodness, and bring you to everlasting life; through Jesus Christ our Lord. *Amen.* (*The Book of Common Prayer*, 332)

There are too many Christians today who think a robust time of communion is intrusive in the Sunday service, or that it cuts down on the words of the preacher. The Lord's Supper is worship. The Lord's Supper is the word of God speaking to us about his Son. The Lord's Supper invites us to enter into the Great High Priest's unfailing love and grace and empowerment and intercession.

Finally, the Instructor turns to positive rather than

comparative terms about Jesus and his eternally redeeming great high priesthood (7:26–28). The Instructor's thoughts are rooted in the work of the high priest on the Day of Atonement (Leviticus 16). He:

1. meets our need,
2. is holy,
3. is blameless,
4. is pure,
5. is set apart from sinners,
6. is exalted above the heavens,
7. does not need to offer sacrifices for himself or daily for others,
8. sacrificed for the sins of others,
9. sacrificed once for all, and
10. sacrificed by offering himself (all in Hebrews 7:26–27).

Following this flourish of attributes of Jesus and his priestly work, the Instructor reminds us of the virtues of new covenant priesthood in Jesus. There is the promissory oath of God, this oath reshapes the law, this oath was given to the Son, and this Son—notice this connection of terms—he was "made perfect" so he could be a priest for us "forever" (7:28). No Levite priest was like this. No law of Moses was like this. Jesus alone is the High Priest like this. He alone redeems us from our sins and waywardness, and he alone empowers us to walk toward him and so enter into the holy place where he is.

I have said this a few times but it's worth repeating: Many, if not most of us, do not live our Christian lives in a world of priestly ministries. This Sermon perhaps will inform us that we actually do live in that world even if we are not aware of it. Each baptism and each communion service remind us of the world we read about in Hebrews. So, even though the thought-world of Hebrews for many today is not only different and unaccommodating and even alienating, that thought-world is the heart of our gospel. I have continued to emphasize one theme that can help the Instructor's words connect with us: The ultimate goal is the Rest, or the kingdom of God, and the discipleship requirement is faithfulness that is long, and this long faithfulness leads to the Rest, and both Rest and long faithfulness is the Perfection the Instructor has in mind. We live out the message of Hebrews when we follow Jesus today. One day at a time. For a lifetime. Long faithfulness. Perfection. All because Jesus is our Pioneer and Perfecter (12:2). And nothing embodies what Jesus has done for us more than the Eucharist we share with one another.

Let's close in prayer, as if we are approaching the Lord's supper:

> Lord Jesus Christ, we humbly thank you that you did choose bread and wine to be the emblems of your sacred Body and Blood, given on the cross for the sins of the world, and did command us thus to remember you. Deepen our repentance, strengthen our faith, and increase our love for one another, that, eating and drinking the sacrament of our redemption, we may truly feed on you in our hearts with thanksgiving, for the sake of your great and worthy name. (John R. W. Stott, amended slightly; from Colquhoun, *Parish Prayers*, 219–220)

QUESTIONS FOR REFLECTION AND APPLICATION

1. What is the difference between the expected job of a prophet and the expected job of a priest?

2. What is the key aspect of the comparison between Jesus and Melchizedek that the Instructor makes?

3. How can Melchizedek be considered greater than Abraham and Moses?

4. How does the Eucharist remind us of both Jesus' redemption and intercession?

5. How often does your tradition celebrate the Eucharist? In what ways can this reading today help you live in a "priestly" reality even if you are not part of a "priestly" or liturgical church tradition?

FOR FURTHER READING

The Book of Common Prayer (New York: Oxford University Press, 1990).

Frank Colquhoun, compiler and editor, *Parish Prayers* (London: Hodder and Stoughton, 2000).

THE SON'S LONG FAITHFULNESS AND THE JESUS-COVENANT

Hebrews 8:1–13

¹ Now the main point of what we are saying is this: We do have such a high priest, who sat down at the right hand of the throne of the Majesty in heaven, ² and who serves in the sanctuary, the true tabernacle set up by the Lord, not by a mere human being.

³ Every high priest is appointed to offer both gifts and sacrifices, and so it was necessary for this one also to have something to offer. ⁴ If he were on earth, he would not be a priest, for there are already priests who offer the gifts prescribed by the law. ⁵ They serve at a sanctuary that is a copy and shadow of what is in heaven. This is why Moses was warned when he was about to build the tabernacle: "See to it that you make everything according to the pattern shown you on the mountain." ⁶ But in fact the ministry Jesus has received is as superior to theirs as the covenant of which he is mediator is superior to the old one, since the new covenant is established on better promises.

⁷ For if there had been nothing wrong with that first covenant, no place would have been sought for another. ⁸ But God found fault with the people and said:

"The days are coming, declares the Lord,
    when I will make a new covenant
with the people of Israel
    and with the people of Judah.
⁹ *It will not be like the covenant*
    I made with their ancestors
when I took them by the hand
    to lead them out of Egypt,
because they did not remain faithful to my covenant,
    and I turned away from them,
    declares the Lord.
¹⁰ *This is the covenant I will establish with the people*
    of Israel
    after that time, declares the Lord.
I will put my laws in their minds
    and write them on their hearts.
I will be their God,
    and they will be my people.
¹¹ *No longer will they teach their neighbor,*
    or say to one another, 'Know the Lord,'
because they will all know me,
    from the least of them to the greatest.
¹² *For I will forgive their wickedness*
    and will remember their sins no more."

¹³ *By calling this covenant "new," he has made the first one obsolete; and what is obsolete and outdated will soon disappear.*

At this point in our reading of Hebrews, one can fairly ask if this is not getting a little long for a sermon. Which reminds me of a Scandinavian story. The stereotypical man, Ole, after the sermon, says to his pastor, "Yew know, Rev'rend, a good sermon should have a good beginning and a good ending—and dey should be as close together as possible!" (Thorud, *Second Best*, 28). The Instructor, I trust, smiles on us in overhearing Ole, who in this case has a case. After all, the Instructor opens our eighth chapter with words that will be his topic from 8:1 through 10:18: "Now the main point of what we are saying is this: We do have such a high priest" (8:1). I translate this as "The header upon what is being said" (*Second Testament*), and Amy Peeler translates it as "And the headline of the things said is this" (Peeler, *Hebrews*, 209). The word "such" in 8:1 refers back to the order of Melchizedek fulfilled perfectly in Jesus: exalted, eternal, and effectively saving. The Instructor wants to begin with Jesus because he knows he's about to get into the weeds about covenants and how they are formed.

We will need to remind ourselves to keep Jesus in mind. Today's passage emphasizes two truths about Jesus: He alone is our Great High Priest, and his priestly ministry occurs, as a result of his ascension, in the presence of the Father in the heavens and its eternal temple (8:1–2). This means *we have access to God in a Person who represents us*. That he "sat down" means he has finished everything he needed to do in order to assume his ministry as the great, eternal high priest (cf. 1:3, 13; 8:1; 10:12; 12:2). As Gareth Cockerill reminds us, we need to keep the fullness of Jesus' high priesthood in mind:

> This is the high priest "appropriate" for our needs. This is the high priest who enables our perseverance. This is the high priest through which we draw near to God in order to find the "mercy" of forgiveness and the "grace" for obedience (Heb 4:16). This is the high priest who has opened "the new and living way" (Heb 10:20). This high priest alone is the "Pioneer and Perfecter of the [way of] faith" (Heb 12:1–3), the one who will sustain us until we reach "Mount Zion" (Heb 12:22–24). (Cockerill, *Hebrews*, 74)

The ultimate goal, again, is for us to enter into the Rest (or the kingdom of God). To get into that Rest, we need to walk in a long faithfulness. We know our weaknesses and that we cannot get there on our own. But Jesus is the Pioneer who was perfected by his own long faithfulness. He sits at the right hand of God interceding for us so we can be empowered to journey as we ought to. Let us learn to trust the power of our Great High Priest who intercedes for us.

This section of Hebrews articulates a singular reshaping of how faith in Jesus relates to the covenant God made with Moses. How Christians have stated this relationship has damaged our relationship with Judaism and Jews all over the world. The Instructor creates a gap between the Christian faith and Judaism, and we will do our best to speak of it with grace and clarity.

COVENANT, LAW, AND PRIESTS

The term *covenant* (*diathēkē*) first appeared in Hebrews 7:22 with Jesus becoming the "guarantor of a better covenant." The style of the Instructor is to drop a term and then pick it up for discussion some verses later. Chapter eight is where the discussion occurs, and we need to define some technical terms to help us make sense of the Instructor.

A *covenant* forms an official relationship, with terms of agreement and obligation, between parties.

A *testament* is a unilateral enactment while a covenant is a bilateral agreement.

However, the new covenant of Hebrews has a testamentary disposition because God arranges the covenant in a unilateral manner (cf. 9:16, 17, 20). Furthermore, God forms a covenant with Abraham on the basis of the promise God made to

Abraham (Genesis 12; 15; 17; 22). So, while some like to sum all this up with the term *covenant* and others with *promise* and yet others with *testament*, I think it's best to sum it up with a double word. A *promissory covenant* accurately frames God's relationship with God's people. The Jesus-covenant brings to completion the original covenant with its promise.

Covenant entails obligation, and the preeminent obligation of the covenant God made with Abraham and then with Moses is the law, which included participation in the tabernacle (and later the temple) with its high priestly order with its "gifts and sacrifices" (7:12, 28; 8:3). The Instructor teaches us to tie these terms into a bundle: promise, covenant, law, priesthood, tabernacle, and temple. As one goes, so goes the others. Jesus' priesthood, being of a different order, reveals that the "sanctuary" formed under Moses is a "copy and shadow" of the eternal form "in heaven" (8:5–6). The earthly tabernacle and temple are earthly representations of the ultimate temple in heaven.

COVENANT, PROMISE, AND JESUS

The Instructor's theology requires some knowledge of how the temple and high priesthood worked. The connections he makes with Jesus, however, are not the abstract theologizing one finds in academic books or in classrooms. No, the connections are all made for a singular purpose: to elevate Jesus as the one who was both perfected by his long faithfulness and who makes our long faithfulness possible because of the completion of the covenant.

Again, these items are a package arrangement: promise, covenant, law, priesthood, tabernacle, and temple. The promissory, oath-established covenant God makes with Jesus as the "mediator" is *better* than the one made with Moses. The Greek terms that matter most in the Jesus-covenant are translated with "superior" and "better." The NIV's "superior" translates both *diaphoros*, which has the sense of "much better" and hence the NIV's choice. But the second use of "superior" and then their word "better" translate another, but the same, Greek term (*kreittōn*). In finessing our English translations, let us not miss the weight of what is intended: The covenant God makes with Jesus is both better and much better than the former covenant. The impact of the Jesus-covenant is a better "ministry" (NIV) or "public work" (*Second Testament*). Jesus is the sole "mediator" of this "new" covenant because the new covenant is founded on "better promises" (8:6). The NIV's "superior to the *old one*" adds the words in italics, anticipating what will be said in 8:13 ("obsolete and outdated"; *Second Testament* has "ancient and old [is] close to vanishing").

The Instructor claims the covenant with Jesus improves upon, expands, extends, and so perfects the Abrahamic and Mosaic arrangements. Even more, he claims there was something "fallible" about the former with an infallibility in the new covenant (8:7; *Second Testament*). What was fallible was not the promise or the covenant that put the promise into effect. What was fallible was what that original covenant effected in the people who were obligated to that covenant. The Instructor quotes Jeremiah 31:31–34, the famous promise of a coming new covenant. In his citation the emphasis shifts from the promise to the arrival of the new covenant, and even more, from the location of the law outside the people to inside the people. But we should pause here to observe that the new people of the new covenant enter into a long faithfulness only because Jesus himself lived that long faithfulness and so was perfected (see sidebar: "The Meaning of Perfection in Hebrews," pp. 108–109).

The former arrangement did not lead to a long faithfulness, as the wilderness story made clear in 3:7–4:13. In the new covenant as predicted in Jeremiah, with a new high priest, mediator, law, and temple, God writes the law "in their minds" and "on their hearts" and they "will all know me, from the least of them to the greatest," and in so regenerating them from the inside-out, God both forgives their sins and promises never to remember them (8:10–12). The passage in Jeremiah 31 echoes Deuteronomy (6:6; 10:16; 11:18; 30:2, 10, 14). The New Testament authors speak in different ways about this work of inner transformation. The book of Acts, chapter two, details the work of the Spirit coming upon us to empower us with gifts. The apostle Paul not only develops the theme of giftedness (1 Corinthians 12–14), but he speaks of the Spirit empowering us to do God's will in the power of the Spirit (Galatians 5:16–25; Romans 6:17–20; 8:1–4). The author of 1 John routinely connects our life in God and God in us. These are complementary beliefs in that each affirms exactly what Jeremiah predicted: an inner work of the Spirit to empower us to do God's will. That is, to complete the journey of a long faithfulness.

This new covenant then makes the former covenant "ancient," not because it was malformed but in the sense that it has grown old and is "close to vanishing" *because Jesus has become the Pioneer and Perfecter* (8:13; *Second Testament*; also 12:2). The impact here is one of *development* of what is already in place rather than *replacing by tossing the former in the garbage*. Christians have a nasty habit of speaking of the Old Testament with its covenant and laws as primitive, forgettable, and no longer useful. But that completely fails Jesus, Paul, Peter, John, James, and the Instructor of this Sermon. The former covenant becomes in the new covenant all God had designed for that former covenant. The new does not eradicate the former. Instead, it expands it to its divinely intended fullness. Here's an image for us to think about: The former covenant provides the infrastructure of the community; the new covenant forms functions, applications, services, and culture. The latter are completely shaped by the former.

The technical discussion here is called *supersessionism*, a term that refers to replacing the Abrahamic-Mosaic covenant with the Jesus covenant in a way that erases the former—in particular, with the church replacing Israel as the people of God. But the people of God to whom the promise of Jeremiah is given is "Israel" and "Judah" (8:8). Such a position of the church radically replacing Israel is "harsh supersessionism" (Pierce, "Hebrews," 596), and it has led over and over to violence against Jews and anti-Semitism. Of course, the Instructor believes the former covenant did not accomplish the fullness that alone was completed in the salvation provided in Christ. Instead of a harsh supersessionism, we are better off referring to *fulfillment*. Or, as Madison Pierce phrases it, we have not a brand-new covenant but a "renewed covenant" (Pierce, "Hebrews," 596). The NIV's terms for former covenant are both "obsolete," when the term is better translated "ancient" (*palaioō*), and "will soon disappear," when the Greek text has no verb and, as such, implies not a future "will" but a present "is." The final clause then is better translated with "is close to vanishing," which is not the same as promising that it "will" in fact "disappear." The former covenant does not, in fact, disappear. The new outdoes the former, for sure, but the former remains the infrastructure of the new. The former is not replaced by tossing it out; the former is the foundation and structure for the (re)new(ed) covenant. Christians are grafted into the story of Israel and so join in the covenant God made with Israel. God did not make a different covenant but renewed the former covenant. Christians do not start a new story; they enter an existing story.

QUESTIONS FOR REFLECTION AND APPLICATION

1. How does it impact you to read: "We have access to God in a Person who represents us"?

2. What does it mean that Jesus has "sat down" as High Priest?

3. How are covenants and testaments different?

4. In what ways does the ancient covenant differ from the renewed, better covenant?

5. What are some ideas you can keep in mind when discussing the old covenant, Jews, and Judaism in order to avoid supersessionism or anti-Semitism?

FOR FURTHER READING

Richard Thorud, editor, *The Second Best of Ole and Lena* (Bloomington, Minnesota: Elliot House, 2007). Thanks to my friend Ben Tertin for this.

THE SON'S LONG FAITHFULNESS AND HIS SACRIFICE

Hebrews 9:1–28

[1] *Now the first covenant had regulations for worship and also an earthly sanctuary.* [2] *A tabernacle was set up. In its first room were the lampstand and the table with its consecrated bread; this was called the Holy Place.* [3] *Behind the second curtain was a room called the Most Holy Place,* [4] *which had the golden altar of incense and the gold-covered ark of the covenant. This ark contained the gold jar of manna, Aaron's staff that had budded, and the stone tablets of the covenant.* [5] *Above the ark were the cherubim of the Glory, overshadowing the atonement cover. But we cannot discuss these things in detail now.*

[6] *When everything had been arranged like this, the priests entered regularly into the outer room to carry on their ministry.* [7] *But only the high priest entered the inner room, and that only once a year, and never without blood, which he offered for himself and for the sins the people had committed in ignorance.* [8] *The Holy Spirit was showing by this that the way into the Most Holy Place had not yet been disclosed as long as the first tabernacle was still*

functioning. [9] This is an illustration for the present time, indicating that the gifts and sacrifices being offered were not able to clear the conscience of the worshiper. [10] They are only a matter of food and drink and various ceremonial washings—external regulations applying until the time of the new order.

[11] But when Christ came as high priest of the good things that are now already here, he went through the greater and more perfect tabernacle that is not made with human hands, that is to say, is not a part of this creation. [12] He did not enter by means of the blood of goats and calves; but he entered the Most Holy Place once for all by his own blood, thus obtaining eternal redemption. [13] The blood of goats and bulls and the ashes of a heifer sprinkled on those who are ceremonially unclean sanctify them so that they are outwardly clean. [14] How much more, then, will the blood of Christ, who through the eternal Spirit offered himself unblemished to God, cleanse our consciences from acts that lead to death, so that we may serve the living God!

[15] For this reason Christ is the mediator of a new covenant, that those who are called may receive the promised eternal inheritance—now that he has died as a ransom to set them free from the sins committed under the first covenant.

[16] In the case of a will, it is necessary to prove the death of the one who made it, [17] because a will is in force only when somebody has died; it never takes effect while the one who made it is living. [18] This is why even the first covenant was not put into effect without blood. [19] When Moses had proclaimed every command of the law to all the people, he took the blood of calves, together with water, scarlet wool and branches of hyssop, and sprinkled the scroll and all the people. [20] He said, "This is the blood of the covenant, which God has commanded you to keep." [21] In the same way, he sprinkled with the blood both the tabernacle and everything used in its ceremonies. [22] In fact, the law requires that nearly everything be cleansed with blood, and without the shedding of blood there is no forgiveness.

²³ It was necessary, then, for the copies of the heavenly things to be purified with these sacrifices, but the heavenly things themselves with better sacrifices than these. ²⁴ For Christ did not enter a sanctuary made with human hands that was only a copy of the true one; he entered heaven itself, now to appear for us in God's presence. ²⁵ Nor did he enter heaven to offer himself again and again, the way the high priest enters the Most Holy Place every year with blood that is not his own. ²⁶ Otherwise Christ would have had to suffer many times since the creation of the world. But he has appeared once for all at the culmination of the ages to do away with sin by the sacrifice of himself. ²⁷ Just as people are destined to die once, and after that to face judgment, ²⁸ so Christ was sacrificed once to take away the sins of many; and he will appear a second time, not to bear sin, but to bring salvation to those who are waiting for him.

A long faithfulness expects different commitments for each of us. At the base level, God expects us to follow Jesus, who himself followed the law of Moses. The Sermon on the Mount's famous chapter five articulates Jesus' interactions with how the law of Moses was being read in his day. He offers some counter-interpretations, but his interpretations are of the law of Moses. Long faithfulness remains yoked to the instruction, which is another translation of *torah*/law, of Moses. Deuteronomy, for instance, instructs and warns the children of Israel to live justly with one another. Justice prohibits violence against one another. Justice work requires a long faithfulness. Perhaps you find yourself wearing down in working for justice. Say, working against racism or unjust wages or human trafficking or systemic prejudices. You may feel you are not making any progress, and you may just want to go home, find another calling, and give up the fight.

Clarence Jordan might stir courage in you to carry on. Jordan translated the New Testament and, true to his purpose to make the Word of God clear for Southerners trapped in and fighting against racism, is now titled *Clarence Jordan's Cotton Patch Gospel*. Here I cite from an essay I wrote about Jordan, and in the essay I quote from Frederick Downing's study of Jordan and words from Leonora Tubbs Tisdale about Jordan:

> The Cotton Patch renditions also influenced Jordan himself, in a way that will be familiar to most writers. Downing explains:
>
> During the writing project, Jordan wrote himself toward a deeper sense of prophetic awareness. Jordan responded to the death of Martin Luther King, Jr., with renewed and deeper commitment. His prophetic vision began to find focus in a critique of American Evangelical Christianity. The journey to radical faith culminated for Jordan in the establishment of Koinonia Partners and a more economic reading of the Bible which called for a redistribution of wealth and the building of partnership houses for the poor. This was essentially Jordan's new covenant idea, no longer simply with the South but with humanity.
>
> Downing's view is confirmed by homiletician Leonora Tubbs Tisdale, whose teaching at Yale Divinity School has focused on contextual preaching and prophetic preaching. She sums up Jordan in these terms . . . "Frankly, I can think of no one who embodies *both* of those aspects of preaching better than Clarence Jordan." (McKnight, "Making")

Nothing in my memory has been as challenging as systemic racism in the USA. Nothing discourages the pursuit of justice more than defeats followed by more defeats. Yet, Jordan himself met a lifetime of such challenges and carried on with a long faithfulness like few others in American history. He faced those challenges with strength because he knew God in the face of Jesus was against the injustices of racism.

The Instructor knows believers face unclimbable and even dangerous systemic walls. He knows they need more than a warning not to give up; they need to know God is with them. Today's reading provides the very source they needed (and we need): Jesus, the great high priest who intercedes for his people to live out what God has called them to live out. David deSilva expresses that situation so very well. The congregants "were finding the pressures of their neighbors too much to bear in the long run and . . . were faltering in their hope for God's future benefits." So, they heard a call "for staying loyal to God, to Jesus, and to the community of faith, whatever the cost in terms of worldly pleasures or hardships" (deSilva, *Hebrews*, 89).

The Instructor, in discussing the brilliance of our Great High Priest (Jesus), observed that Jesus did not need to offer a sacrifice for his own sins, and neither did he need to make sacrifices daily or annually for those he redeems. Rather, Jesus "sacrificed for their sins once for all when he offered himself" (7:27). Recall that the One who here offers himself for our sins is God's Son, the creator and heir of all, and is the "radiance of God's glory and the exact representation of his being" (1:1–4). His sacrifice secures an "eternal salvation" (5:9). In offering himself, Jesus formed a new covenant (chapter eight) and an eternal redemption (today's reading). This was the empowerment the believers needed.

Once again, the Instructor compares the original covenant made with Abraham and Moses to the renewed covenant with God's Son. The sections of today's reading are easy to distinguish: The redemption of the first covenant (9:1–10) is followed by the redemption of the new covenant with Christ (9:11–28). It is only by understanding the covenant redemption under Moses that we can understand the covenant redemption under Christ.

COVENANT REDEMPTION

Covenants include promises and obligations, and to participate in a covenant, like signing a legal contract with notarized witnesses, entails some "regulations" that govern both the relationship and appropriate behaviors. A liturgical church forms its relationship with a book of order, which shapes Sunday morning worship, the conduct of weddings and funerals, and the proper words for special occasions. Denominations have formed their own book of order, so the Methodists and the Presbyterians and the Episcopalians all have a book of order. They are rooted in the original covenant we now read in Deuteronomy, which we could say is the original book of order for worship and conduct. At the heart of that book of order was a sacrificial system in the tabernacle (and then later the temple).

The "first" covenant occurred in an "earthly sanctuary," and here the Instructor is talking about the "tabernacle" in the wilderness journey from Egypt to the promised land. That tabernacle, with its two major sections, looked something like the example on the following page.

A diagram of the tabernacle can be found on page 131.

The Instructor walks us through the structure of the tabernacle. The Holy Place included the lampstand and the table with consecrated bread. The Most Holy Place included the golden altar of incense and the ark of the covenant, in which could be found a gold jar of manna, the budded staff of

Aaron, and the stone tablets of the covenant itself. Above the ark were the cherubim that were "overshadowing the mercy seat" (9:5; *Second Testament*). Due either to time or space, the Instructor says he is unable to "discuss these things in detail now" (9:5). To the priests were assigned the duties of worship in the tabernacle's Holy Place, but only the high priest entered the Most Holy Place, and even then, only once a year with blood for atonement and purification (9:6–7).

This sketch prompts reflection and interpretation of the significance of the tabernacle. Let's reflect for a moment on words we use for the tabernacle. We use terms like "symbolic" or even "emblematic" for the tabernacle, and such terms echo the term used by the Instructor. He prefers "copy" and "shadow" (8:5; 9:24). If we think of the tabernacle as the infrastructure of the new covenant's heavenly tabernacle, we might think, too, of the earthly tabernacle as an icon. Icons invigorate our imaginations to wander into the truths those icons display. Icons are two-dimensional and so cannot display the fullness of someone or something. The tabernacle can be seen as iconic by the Instructor because of

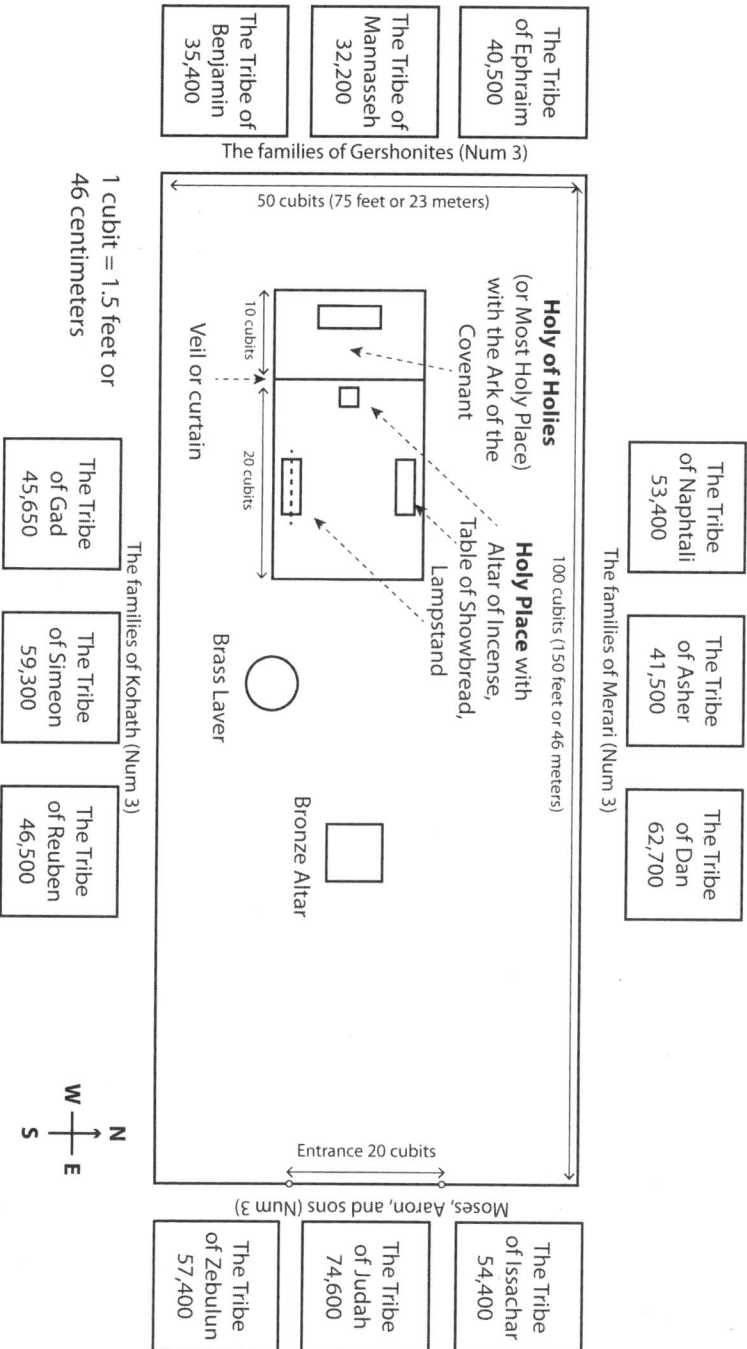

The families of Gershonites (Num 3)

The Tribe of Ephraim 40,500

The Tribe of Mannasseh 32,200

The Tribe of Benjamin 35,400

1 cubit = 1.5 feet or 46 centimeters

50 cubits (75 feet or 23 meters)

Holy of Holies (or Most Holy Place) with the Ark of the Covenant

10 cubits

Veil or curtain

20 cubits

Holy Place with Altar of Incense, Table of Showbread, Lampstand

100 cubits (150 feet or 46 meters)

Brass Laver

Bronze Altar

The families of Kohath (Num 3)

The Tribe of Gad 45,650

The Tribe of Simeon 59,300

The Tribe of Reuben 46,500

The families of Merari (Num 3)

The Tribe of Naphtali 53,400

The Tribe of Asher 41,500

The Tribe of Dan 62,700

Entrance 20 cubits

N W S E

Moses, Aaron, and sons (Num 3)

The Tribe of Issachar 54,400

The Tribe of Judah 74,600

The Tribe of Zebulun 57,400

131

its two-dimensionality; it is not the fullness. Yet, it is more than symbolic and iconic because it remains the infrastructure of the sacrifice of Christ. Flipped around, the tabernacle iconically reveals Christ's own tabernacle.

The Instructor's interpretation reflects belief that the Holy Spirit revealed the ultimate plan of eternal redemption in Christ in that original tabernacle (9:8). His point, which requires making earlier connections in this Sermon, was that the once-a-year entry and sacrifice, and the restrictions for both priests and the high priest, meant that the entrance into the presence of God for all people at all times was still a future reality. At that time, only the high priest knew what the Most Holy Place looked like. It was hidden from view even to other priests. The Most Holy Place in today's reading works in three ways:

1. It is an earthly reality in the tabernacle.
2. It is a heavenly reality that is the ultimate reality.
3. Believers can enter into that heavenly reality now (9:9).

That heavenly reality was stated also at 8:2: "The sanctuary, the true tabernacle" is where Jesus sat down as the Great High Priest. Jesus opened the way for *all of us* into that eternal Most Holy Place (10:20). Madison Pierce draws out the significance of this for today when she writes that the heavenly sanctuary "is a space for *us*. Historic divisions among the people of God are eliminated. Further, this privileged place of priestly service is not restricted to a particular class, a particular ethnicity, or a particular gender." She gets real with, "Those who have been asked to 'remain silent in the churches,' and those who have been seated in their own sections, the balconies, or sent to their 'own' churches across the town, they enter the holiest space with every benefit of God's promise" (Pierce, "Hebrews," 597). All of this is packed into the "all of us" words above.

Because the earthly sanctuary's holy places were both restricted and repeated, an eternal, once-for-all redemption was not effected in the tabernacle. Those sacrifices took care of purity at the earthly level (9:9–10). They are, in the Instructor's term, an "illustration" (9:9), or better yet, an "analogy" (*Second Testament*), which is the same term used for "parables" in the Gospels (*parabolē*; Peeler translates it as "parable" here; *Hebrews*, 230). Parables are more than illustrations. They draw a person into a story to develop message and meaning through imagery and metaphor. They become iconic when we enter into them.

RENEWED COVENANT REDEMPTION

With the infrastructure of the heavenly tabernacle provided in the earthly tabernacle, the Instructor puts up walls and places furniture that reveal the atonement effected by our great high priest, Christ. We should think a bit again of what a priest was, and I turn to the words of Eugene Peterson, who once wrote these words about what a priest is and does:

> A priest is a connector, one who establishes living connections between persons and their meanings. A priest puts things together for a person—things that have to do with the world, with humanity, and with God. A priest acts as a kind of repairer of relationships. Where there have been mangled connections, short circuits, and ill-fitting joints, he tries to get everything to fit and connect again. (Peterson, *Lights a Lovely Mile*, 110)

Many items are placed in the heavenly tabernacle, and they all fit together because the priests know what to do at each location with each item. Jesus, too, performs priestly actions. He establishes redemptive "good things" that "are now already here" by passing through the eternal tabernacle (9:11). Then he offers his own blood and not that of "goats and calves" (9:12), and here blood signifies a life given (death) to bring life to others. Because Jesus is the eternal One, because he offered himself "through the eternal Spirit," and because he was "unblemished" by sin, his blood secures "eternal redemption" (9:12–14, 15; cf. 4:15). The redemption Jesus provides, however, transcends forgiveness of sins. He can "cleanse our consciences," but his atoning work empowers us to "serve the living God" (9:14). Here we are led one more time to the formative power of God's redemption in Christ: We are being empowered for a long faithfulness. The hymn "There Is a Green Hill Far Away," written by one who lived out a life of grace and justice for all, opens its third verse with these two lines: "He died that we might be forgiv'n/ He died to make us good (Cecil Frances Alexander)." This perfectly sums up Hebrews 9:14.

The Instructor does not want his congregants to give up or lose hope. Because of *who Jesus is and what Jesus has accomplished* as the "mediator of a new covenant," we are led by him into "the promised eternal inheritance" (9:15). This inheritance is the Rest of chapters three and four. The redemptive work of our Great High Priest not only cleanses but it transforms, and in that transformation comes the power for a long faithfulness. Let us carry on, then, in the work of justice in the power of our Great High Priest.

A long footnote follows in Hebrews 9:16–22, and it clarifies why a death—that is, blood—is necessary. The Instructor now turns more to the idea of a testament, or a "will" (9:16), which does not go into effect until the testator dies (9:17–22). The covenant with Moses required such a death (designated by "blood"), but notice the intent of this blood: *purification or cleansing* (9:22). Moses was instructed to purify the scroll (Exodus 24:4), the people, the tabernacle, and all the items in the tabernacle. Forgiveness, then, is a cleansing or purification so a person can enter the presence of God. If Moses purified everything and everyone, how much more did Christ purify all of creation and all of us? His sacrifice was "better" (Hebrews 9:23) because, in a once-for-all-time offering, he purified us for the eternal presence of God (9:24–26).

Notice the logic of a verse many of us committed to memory at some point:

A Just as people are destined to die once,
   B and after that to face judgment.
A So Christ was sacrificed once
   B to take away the sins of many.

The logic of 9:27 puts our facing "judgment" to be something Jesus himself endured for our sake by removing what would condemn us. Tying his thoughts now to the final Rest, or inheritance, or kingdom of God, the Instructor informs his congregation that Jesus will "appear a second time." The Second Coming is not to remove sin but to bring final "salvation to those who are waiting for him" in a long faithfulness (9:28). The "salvation" of which he speaks is that Rest.

Jesus accomplishes this salvation; we do not. Jesus lived out a long faithfulness and so was perfected and exalted to the right hand of God. There, he intercedes for us so that we can journey forward on the road of a long faithfulness. He is the Pioneer and Perfecter, and so empowers us to live faithfully, fighting daily for justice in the power God grants us.

Questions for Reflection and Application

1. How can Jesus' obedience to the law of Moses inspire our obedience to God today?

2. In what ways does the tabernacle serve as an icon of Jesus' sacrifice?

3. What priestly actions does Jesus perform?

4. What makes you feel weary in working for justice?

5. How do you need Jesus' priestly mediation in your life to help you keep walking faithfully?

FOR FURTHER READING

Cecil Frances Alexander, "There Is a Green Hill
    Far Away," https://hymnary.org/text/there_is_a
    _green_hill_far_away.
Scot McKnight, "The Making of a Redemptive
    Subversive," *Christian Century* 135/9 (April,
    2018), 30–33.
Eugene Peterson, *Lights a Lovely Mile: Collected
    Sermons of the Church Year* (Colorado Springs:
    WaterBrook, 2023).

LONG FAITHFULNESS
IS A JOURNEY

Hebrews 10:1–18

[1] The law is only a shadow of the good things that are coming—not the realities themselves. For this reason it can never, by the same sacrifices repeated endlessly year after year, make perfect those who draw near to worship. [2] Otherwise, would they not have stopped being offered? For the worshipers would have been cleansed once for all, and would no longer have felt guilty for their sins. [3] But those sacrifices are an annual reminder of sins. [4] It is impossible for the blood of bulls and goats to take away sins.

[5] Therefore, when Christ came into the world, he said:

> *"Sacrifice and offering you did not desire,*
>   *but a body you prepared for me;*
> *[6] with burnt offerings and sin offerings*
>   *you were not pleased.*
> *[7] Then I said, 'Here I am—it is written about me in*
>   *the scroll—*
> *I have come to do your will, my God.'"*

[8] First he said, "Sacrifices and offerings, burnt offerings and sin offerings you did not desire, nor were you pleased with

them"—though they were offered in accordance with the law. *9 Then he said, "Here I am, I have come to do your will." He sets aside the first to establish the second. *10 And by that will, we have been made holy through the sacrifice of the body of Jesus Christ once for all.

*11 Day after day every priest stands and performs his religious duties; again and again he offers the same sacrifices, which can never take away sins. *12 But when this priest had offered for all time one sacrifice for sins, he sat down at the right hand of God, *13 and since that time he waits for his enemies to be made his footstool. *14 For by one sacrifice he has made perfect forever those who are being made holy.

*15 The Holy Spirit also testifies to us about this. First he says:

> *16 "This is the covenant I will make with them
> after that time, says the Lord.
> I will put my laws in their hearts,
> and I will write them on their minds."

*17 Then he adds:

> "Their sins and lawless acts
> I will remember no more."

*18 And where these have been forgiven, sacrifice for sin is no longer necessary.

Life with God is a journey, which is why in chapters three and four of the book of Hebrews the Instructor chose, as a prototype for followers of Jesus, the wilderness journey of the children of Israel. They were ransomed in Egypt, walked through the Red Sea unharmed, tooled around the wilderness developing some bad habits as they learned to trust God for provisions, received the laws for a long life in the covenant, and journeyed north to the shore of the Jordan

River only to fail the challenge of a long faithfulness. The children of Israel's story of life with God as a journey has been repeated over and over in literature, and I'm thinking of Christian literature, from Augustine's *Confessions* to Dante's *Divine Comedy*, from John Bunyan's *Pilgrim's Progress* to Hannah Hurnard's *Hinds' Feet on High Places*, and from Francine Rivers's Mark of the Lion series to J. R. R. Tolkien's *The Lord of the Rings*.

Journeys well told are stories. Our friend Leslie Fields is a storyteller who teaches folks how to tell their own story (see For Further Reading for more). She says there are five elements of a story: an opening hook that grabs our attention, a vivid outer story that happened in your life, a meaningful inner story that presents a challenge with tensions in need of resolution, an inner story that leads to a new place that can offer insight to the reader, and, all along, the storyteller has to be authentic.

This Sermon in Hebrews is not a story per se, but there is a very clear, vivid outer story (from Egypt to the promised land, from life now to the Final Rest) with a meaningful inner story (you and I living out a long faithfulness with plenty of personal challenges along the path), and—of course—each of us is in need of telling our own story in our own voice to make our story authentic. The Instructor makes abundant use of the failure of one journey as a motivating story to challenge you and me to complete our journeys.

Today's reading creates no less than six separable stories, each of which can be turned into a journey of long faithfulness. But the Instructor does not bark out, "Hey folks, listen up! I want to sketch out six ways to travel through the Christian life." Instead, he puts before all of us what I call the "goal-terms," and we are then invited to consider how to frame the whole story in light of those goal-terms. If you, like the scouts among the children of Israel, want to figure out what's and who's on the horizon, you might shuffle the pages of your Bible to the next chapter of Hebrews to learn about those who did walk the path of a long faithfulness successfully.

The Six Journeys Toward the Final Rest

1. The journey toward perfection
2. The journey toward purification
3. The journey toward holiness
4. The journey toward forgiveness of sins
5. The journey toward total victory
6. The journey toward inner transformation

GOAL-TERMS

We just can't get to the heart of the Instructor's Sermon until we accept that (1) the ultimate goal in life is the Rest, or eternal joy in the presence of God, and (2) we are a problem. We are not only sinners in need of forgiveness, but we have a propensity not to do what God wants. To do God's will, we are in continuous need of empowerment for the long faithfulness; the journey from where we have been and where we are to that Rest. For today's Scripture reading, I'm going to ask you to circle the italicized words in the text at the beginning of this passage or in your Bible, or in both places, and then to draw lines across the page from one word to the next. They are "make perfect" (10:1); "cleansed once for all" (10:2); "sins" (10:3); "to take away sins" (10:4); "made holy" (10:10); "take away sins" (10:11); "one sacrifice for sins" (10:12); "his enemies to be made his footstool" (10:13); "made perfect forever" with "being made holy" (10:14); "I will put my laws in their hearts" and "on their minds" (10:16); "remember no more"

(10:17); and then finally, "forgiven" (10:18). Those are the goal-terms the Instructor's Sermon urges upon his people. He wants them to yearn for and journey toward those conditions, and if they don't want those conditions, they won't be able to enjoy God's blessings.

Each of these terms can be reversed to discover the starting point in the journey that leads to the goal-terms. So, those who begin as imperfect need perfections. Those who begin dirtied by sins need to be cleansed. Those who begin with sin and as sinners need to be forgiven. Those who begin as undevoted to God or separate from God need to be made holy or to be devoted to God. Those who begin without inner work of God need the laws of God to be implanted in them. And those who begin with the burdens of sin journey into forgiveness or being released of their burden.

THE MAP

There was a day when those who journeyed from one location to a distant location needed a map or a collection of maps in the car. Kris and I wore out several bound maps of the entire USA. Today, we use our GPS, and we can even choose the accents of the voices that speak to us over the speaker systems in our car. Recently, we were riding in the car with friends. When he drove, the accent was British, and when she drove, the accent was Australian. Regardless of the tool we use, we need help to get from one location to another, from where we are to the Rest, and the Instructor provides maps for our journey in today's reading. Here are the decisive guidelines.

First, the law of Moses alone will not get us to the Rest (10:1–4). Not because the law is bad, but because the law was an incomplete revelation of God's plan. "Without" the law, "we would have no way of understanding Christ or the blessings he provides" (Cockerill, *Hebrews*, 94). But it's not enough. In the former days, Kris and I had separate maps for each state. A map for Iowa will not help us when we get to Nebraska or to Colorado. If the goal is to navigate the Rockies, we need the right map. The Instructor makes it clear that the law of Moses never could get us to the Rest. It was only a "shadow of the good things," but not in the sense of darkness. No, this shadow is but the preliminary sketch, the infrastructure upon which the revelation in Christ will be formed. That is, in the law we can discern the direction of the Rest, but no more. The law is a glimpse of the "image itself" (*Second Testament*) or the "realities themselves" (10:1, NIV). In fact, the constant need for sacrifices indicated to the worshipers that the tabernacle system did not accomplish a permanent or an eternal redemption but only a temporal redemption (10:2–4).

Second, listen to Christ alone (speaking in 10:5–7); he alone can get us to the Rest because Christ alone lived long faithfulness perfectly (10:5–10). The great news is that you and I, once we begin the journey, realize quickly that not only is the path difficult but that we will never make it. We need the redemption that is fully effective in removing sin and its deathly destructions, and in today's reading Jesus is that effective sacrifice (10:10, 12, 14; cf. 9:23–28). We need the path to be clear, the provisions to sustain us, and the strength to make it. Christ is the path, the provisions, and the strength. The best news ever for our journey can be found in the word of Jesus when he entered this world and made his commitment to the Father's map for his journey of long faithfulness. Jesus said, "Here I am . . . I have come to do your will, my God" (10:7, citing Psalm 40:6–8). This is why the Instructor calls Jesus the Pioneer of our long faithfulness (Hebrews 2:10; 12:2). He took the law of Moses to its goal, transcended the law, and personalized the entire will of God onto himself (10:7, 9–10). That very "will" of God that Jesus chose to do for us makes *us* holy in his "sacrifice . . . once for all" (10:10).

Third, Christ's work is not done until the Rest (10:11–14). You and I may have grown up learning that we are *already saved*, but some of us have struggled knowing if we were one of the elect. I know I grew up wondering if I was saved; then I received Christ and knew I *was saved*; then I wandered from that as a teen and wondered if I *had even been saved*; then I devoted my life to Christ and became convinced again that I *was saved*. But the Instructor, just like Jesus, Paul, Peter, James, and John, knows that salvation is both a now and a not-yet reality. Which is why the Instructor informs us that Christ's work is not completely done until . . . here's how he puts it: "since that time" when Christ offered himself until now "he waits for his enemies to be made his footstool" (10:13). His one sacrifice of himself "has made perfect forever" the believers, but they are also in the present "being made holy" (10:14) until that final day when the victory is achieved and the Rest is entered. In the New Testament we have been saved, we are being saved, and we will be saved: three integrated moments on our journey to the Rest.

Old Covenant and New Covenant

Old (9:11)	New (9:12)
Every priest	Christ
Stands	Sat down
Ministers daily	
Offers often	Offers once-for-all
Same sacrifices	Himself
Unable to remove sins	Removes sin

Based on Peeler, *Hebrews*, 270

Fourth, the Spirit of God, who is talking in verses fifteen through seventeen, illuminates and empowers us in the journey to the Rest (10:15–18). Previously, I wrote, "We need the path to be clear, the provisions to sustain us, and the strength to make it. Christ is the path, the provisions, and the strength." Now, we add the Spirit: Christ sets the path, provides the provisions, and strengthens us *through the Holy Spirit* who transforms us, and the Spirit illuminates the path and empowers us to keep on the path of this long faithfulness.

These four guidelines, or signs, on the journey, which we can see daily in our journeys, remind us that the goal of our journey is perfection, purification, holiness, forgiveness, final victory, and an ongoing work of inner transformation. The journey is complex, because we can view it from each of these goal terms. The journey is also simple: Today, we walk forward, with Christ as our Pioneer, with the Spirit empowering us, one step at a time. We can't take tomorrow's steps today. We don't know what tomorrow brings. What we do know is Christ is right in front of us.

QUESTIONS FOR REFLECTION
AND APPLICATION

1. How did the Israelites fail in their journey?

2. Look at the italicized words (the goal-terms) in the verses of Hebrews 10:1–18 and write each of them next to one of the six journeys listed in the sidebar on page 141. Add the Bible verse reference after the italicized terms. What do you observe or learn from doing this exercise?

3. How does Jesus serve as our map for the journey?

4. Which of the goal-terms do you most need in your life?

5. Consider Leslie Fields' five elements of a story. Reflect on your own journey through life and faith. Where would you identify those elements in your story?

FOR FURTHER READING

For Leslie Leyland Fields, who lives in Kodiak Alaska, see: https://www.leslieleylandfields.com/.

AN EXHORTATION TO LONG FAITHFULNESS #4

Hebrews 10:19–39

[19] *Therefore, brothers and sisters, since we have confidence to enter the Most Holy Place by the blood of Jesus,* [20] *by a new and living way opened for us through the curtain, that is, his body,* [21] *and since we have a great priest over the house of God,* [22] *let us draw near to God with a sincere heart and with the full assurance that faith brings, having our hearts sprinkled to cleanse us from a guilty conscience and having our bodies washed with pure water.* [23] *Let us hold unswervingly to the hope we profess, for he who promised is faithful.* [24] *And let us consider how we may spur one another on toward love and good deeds,* [25] *not giving up meeting together, as some are in the habit of doing, but encouraging one another—and all the more as you see the Day approaching.*

[26] *If we deliberately keep on sinning after we have received the knowledge of the truth, no sacrifice for sins is left,* [27] *but only a fearful expectation of judgment and of raging fire that will consume the enemies of God.* [28] *Anyone who rejected the law of Moses died without mercy on the testimony of two or three witnesses.* [29] *How much more severely do you think someone deserves to be*

punished who has trampled the Son of God underfoot, who has treated as an unholy thing the blood of the covenant that sanctified them, and who has insulted the Spirit of grace? [30] For we know him who said, "It is mine to avenge; I will repay," and again, "The Lord will judge his people." [31] It is a dreadful thing to fall into the hands of the living God.

[32] Remember those earlier days after you had received the light, when you endured in a great conflict full of suffering. [33] Sometimes you were publicly exposed to insult and persecution; at other times you stood side by side with those who were so treated. [34] You suffered along with those in prison and joyfully accepted the confiscation of your property, because you knew that you yourselves had better and lasting possessions. [35] So do not throw away your confidence; it will be richly rewarded.

[36] You need to persevere so that when you have done the will of God, you will receive what he has promised. [37] For,

> *"In just a little while,*
> *he who is coming will come*
> *and will not delay."*

[38] And,

> *"But my righteous one will live by faith.*
> *And I take no pleasure*
> *in the one who shrinks back."*

[39] But we do not belong to those who shrink back and are destroyed, but to those who have faith and are saved.

There is a time to encourage, a time to exhort, and a time to warn. The Instructor senses a time to exhort his congregants to a long faithfulness, and with the exhortation to warn them of the consequences of refusing to continue on the path. This is the fourth warning section in the Sermon (2:1–4; 3:7–4:13; 5:11–6:12; 10:19–39, and then 12:4–29; see "The Warning Passages of Hebrews: Themes," p. 31). In our reflection on today's reading, we will synthesize the *consequences* for walking away from the path of a long faithfulness. Remember that each warning passage has four elements: the audience, the sin about which the Instructor is so concerned, the exhortation to a long faithfulness, and the consequences of refusing to continue on the path (see the "Four Elements of the Warning Passages," p. 47).

The Instructor's personal skills are on display in today's reading. Instead of piling warning on top of warning, and instead of resorting to a shrill voice, and rather than choosing to label the people with insulting names, the Instructor pastors his congregation in how he warns. Notice he begins with encouraging affirmations (10:19–25), then warns (10:26–31), and then reminds, exhorts, and affirms (10:32–39). Two sections of affirmation surround the warning. You may have learned the social skill of beginning a letter or a conversation or a meeting with words of affirmation before turning to the more serious matters, and you have learned, too, to finish off the meeting with action points that in some way affirms those who are to accomplish them. That social skill is as old as healthy parenting, pastoring, and working with people.

AFFIRMATION #1: ACCESS TO GOD

The Instructor points us to Christ, not to ourselves. He opens with an affirmation: "Since we have confidence to enter the Most Holy Place by the blood of Jesus," which sums up the redemption provided for us in our great high priest (7:1–10:18). He clarifies the path into the presence of God as a "new and living way," which points us again to Christ as the Pioneer (2:10; 12:2). Entering into the Most Holy Place occurs because the "body" of Jesus is the curtain (10:20). He is our sole access to God. Since "we have" the conviction for entering, he names our access again. We are exhorted to "draw near to God" because, once again, "we have" in Jesus "a great high priest over the house of God" (10:21). The Most Holy Place is now named the "house of God," and we are the family that belongs in that house.

What we perhaps most need in this journey of long faithfulness is confidence (10:19, 35) to keep our heads up and our eyes on Jesus as we enter into God's holy, loving presence. Many believers genuinely believe their sins have been wiped away; they understand that God loves them, that God's grace has been showered upon them, and that God has provided the power for them to carry on with a long faithfulness. But their confidence lags; their convictions are not stirred; and their emotions are not there. The Instructor wants to stir the Spirit in the believers to re-form their confidence that they belong in the presence of God. He is saying to them, *You are right where you belong because you belong here.*

Two more affirmations of what we already have in Christ bolster the Instructor's affirmations and exhortations: "having our hearts sprinkled to cleanse us from a guilty conscience" and "having our bodies washed with pure water" (10:22). Christ has forgiven us; Christ has paved this "new and living way" into the presence of God; let us "draw near" and also "let us hold unswervingly" or "without leaning" away from (10:23; *Second Testament*) the "hope." One more time he offers words of affirmation, this time about God's absolute faithfulness: "for he who promised is faithful" (10:23). If they are not confident yet, they could be.

So, he exhorts those who are created to be in God's presence and to live in the house of God (10:21) to live as a family and fellowship of believers (10:24–25). Their long faithfulness is both God-ward and church-ward. That fellowship will involve (1) "incitement," or an encouraging poke in the ribs or a tap on the shoulder to come along to a life marked by "love and beautiful works" (10:24; *Second Testament*); (2) gathering together with one another; and (3) encouraging each other. Take a long look at these two verses. Are these happening to you when you gather with other believers? Do you experience these on Sunday mornings? Passive pew-sitting creates cultures for those who are there to take in what is offered up front, but are the structures designed for each of us to incite others to do good and to give mutual encouragement? (I'm thinking the Passing of the Peace doesn't get the job done.) Because the ultimate goal is the Rest, and because that Rest follows the final "Day," which implies God's judgment, we are exhorted to give our attention to what spurs one another onward (10:25).

It is easier to instruct Christians to *attend church on Sunday mornings* and thus measure one's church commitment by attendance than it is to form a culture that fosters mutual encouragement and mutual incitement to good works. If the latter is not happening, is it a church? Amy Peeler enters into that question in the following:

> When asked if Christians should attend church, one can answer, on the basis of this verse, with a solid yes. Real life is complicated, and so there may be times for exceptions to the rule, but the ideal presented here is that believers need one another. They need to be known by one another well enough so that both encouragement and provocation can be given and received with wisdom and mutual understanding. On one hand, attending church alone may not fulfill this admonition, for while learning about and praising God with others is vital, if it is done without real

relationship, the singular Christian is left exposed to the deceitfulness of sin because they have no other believers with whom they can dialogue. On the other hand, while Christian friendships can meet the relational need, if they have no tether to a local body of believers, they lack the protection of external accountability. (Peeler, *Hebrews*, 287)

The overall affirmation in today's reading is that we have in Jesus Christ access to God because we have, through his body, broken through the curtain into the innermost House of God. We have this access, not because of what we have done, but because of what God has done for us in Christ. But . . . there is also a time to warn.

WARNING

This fourth warning, which is not long but strong, gives us the opportunity to synthesize what the five warnings teach about the *consequences* for those who choose not to continue in the long faithfulness. Please observe that the Instructor includes himself in this warning, opening with, "If *we* deliberately keep on sinning" (10:26, emphasis added). Using "we" like this speaks a word of "rhetorical solidarity" (Peeler, *Hebrews*, 289). To keep both sides of the ledger in view when we encounter these warnings in this Sermon, the grace and the responsibility sides, we need to hear these words: "With the gift of the knowledge of the truth about God and God's Messiah comes the awesome responsibility of living in light of that truth" (deSilva, *Hebrews*, 91).

So, we turn to the words about this awesome responsibility, to the most important expressions in the Warning passages about possible consequences for those who apostasize from the faith (see 5:11–12). To *apostasize* is to walk away from God (Father, Son, Spirit) and to walk away from the Body of Christ in this world, the fellowship of believers. In today's passage the sin of apostasy is sketched out in graphic imagery in 10:29. Apostasy is a settled disposition in a person who defies God's work that makes people holy, degrades the redemptive work of Jesus, and insults the Spirit of God. The Instructor, we may remember, had asked his congregation a question earlier if any of them should commit apostasy, "How shall we escape?" (2:3), with the implication that there is no escape. He speaks of the consequence of God's "anger" for apostasy (3:10, 17), but most importantly he uses the image of not entering into the Rest (3:11, 18–19; 4:1, 6, 11). He writes about that generation's collapsing in the wilderness/desert (3:17). At the heart of his warning, the Instructor knows that "it is impossible [for apostates] to be brought back to repentance" (6:4–6), and Esau is an example of this (12:16–17). In today's reading, we read of this consequence for those who "deliberately keep on sinning," which is code for refusing to repent and for apostasy (again, 10:29), there is "no sacrifice for sins . . . left" (10:26). He presses his point with the consequence of facing "a fearful expectation of judgment and of raging fire that will consume the enemies of God" (10:27; also 6:8 and 12:29), and that such persons will die outside of God's mercy (10:28) as the consequence of facing God in judgment (10:30–31). Such persons will end up "destroyed" (10:39).

The Instructor warns his audience that people can deliberately, consciously, and proudly walk away from the faith and that such persons will experience final separation from the House of God because they will never enter into the final Rest. If non-entering could occur in the former covenant, it can certainly occur under the new covenant's conditions. David deSilva re-expresses the severity of the Instructor's words in terms we might need to hear today:

The picture of God and the emotions the preacher evokes in regard to God in this paragraph are not popular in twenty-first-century Western Christianity. God is presented as one who holds people accountable for their actions and responses and who visits judgment upon those who have persisted in outrages against God's honor and the honor of the Son. The preacher promotes the fear of God—a deep respect for God's honor and an aversion to the consequences of abusing God's honor—as a good and healthy thing even for Christians to maintain. Many of us shy away from the notion as perhaps too primitive of a view of God, yet our scriptural heritage promotes this understanding rather consistently. (deSilva, *Hebrews*, 99)

He's right. This is a severe warning, and the Instructor will not back down from its severity. As a pastor, however, he is confident that those who hear or read his words are not apostates. He knows apostasy is possible; he thinks better of those he pastors. So, he affirms them again. Gareth Cockerill observes that these words are of no interest to the apostate. Instead, the Instructor knows his audience has not yet abandoned the journey. As he writes, "The pastor would not be warning his hearers if he believed they had come to this terrible end. He is not writing to torment the consciences of the sensitive. The apostate is beyond the reach of conscience. . . . He is putting before his hearers the inevitable end of those who, despite full knowledge of the truth, persist in their neglect of the things of God" (Cockerill, *Hebrews*, 109). We need to remind ourselves and others of this perspective when these passages begin to torment souls. Those who wonder if they have apostatized have no need to wonder. Apostates know what they have done.

AFFIRMATION #2: REMEMBER

With a heavy warning made heavier by the severe consequences, the Instructor turns his heart toward his own people to exhort them, and he does so with three separate exhortations: "Remember," "Do not throw away your confidence," and "You need to persevere" (10:32, 35, 36). He concentrates on urging them to think back over the course of the journey in "those earlier days" (10:32; cf. 5:12). In what we white Americans need to realize, unlike us, these early believers suffered immensely for their faith. The Instructor details their suffering as being "publicly exposed to degradations and troubles." Our African American, Latin American, and Asian American sisters and brothers resonate with the suffering of these early believers. In the USA, some white Christians, as Madison Pierce notes, have mocked the worship styles, preaching, and passion of persons of color (Pierce, "Hebrews," 601). Because of the commitment of the early believers to their church folks, they shared a "common life with those being treated" abusively, including attending to those in prison, and they even "welcomed the plundering of [their] possessions" (10:32–34; *Second Testament*). They need to keep a firm grip on their confidence, which the Instructor knew they had (10:19), and not toss it away by abandoning the path (10:35). One very general term for what the believers needed most to do was "to persevere" (10:36), a term that could be translated as "long faithfulness." The term contrasts with what happened to the children of Israel in the wilderness generation (3:7–4:13), and it is general enough for each of us to fill in our own life's details. We can ask what perseverance looks like for us—today or this week or this month or this year. The same principle abides for all believers: "When you must wait on God, don't lose your faith; *use* your faith!

(Massey-Kaalund, "Hebrews," 483). This is exactly what Hebrews 11 illustrates.

When we are flagging in our devotion, in our struggles for justice or peace or old-fashioned goodness, thinking back over the course of our journey in the faith, not least over those early days when we made fast progress as followers of Jesus, can strengthen our resilience to continue on the path toward the Rest.

In exhorting the believers to remember, to grip their confidence firmly, and to persevere, the Instructor makes a promise that is as good as God: "So that when you have done the will of God, you will receive what he has promised" (10:36). The promise ultimately is the Rest, and to support this promise, the Instructor, instead of straight-up quoting from the Bible, mixes Isaiah 26:20 with Habakkuk 2:3 (Hebrews 10:37–38). The effect is to remind us that the Lord is coming and that we are to live by faith until he comes, with a reminder, too, that the Lord has "no pleasure in the one who shrinks back" (10:38). That word, of course, reminds us all of the consequences the Instructor details in this Sermon.

Finally, he affirms them again, this time identifying himself with the entire congregation. This is a wise pastoral move for him to make at this juncture: "*We* do not belong to those who shrink back and are destroyed." He is sharing his confidence with them as he urges them to resume to live in their confidence (10:19, 35). Rather, he is confident that he and they are "those who have faith and are saved" (10:39). The Instructor's word, however, is not the normal use that is translated with "saved." His words could be translated "for the acquisition of [one's] self" (*Second Testament*). This term often refers to what God possesses (or acquires), as in Ephesians 1:14 and 1 Peter 2:9 when it refers to God's people, but it also can refer to our acquisition of redemptive blessings, like salvation (1 Thessalonians 5:9) or glory (2 Thessalonians 2:14). The Instructor thinks of this acquisition as the final Rest—that is, our acquisition of our inheritance. Now if we just imagine ourselves back with the wilderness generation, we, in the terms of the Instructor, are given a similar, but transcending, offer. As those who entered the land were assigned a lot, or a plot of land, so we, as we stand on the shore, are about to be given our plot of land in the heavenly city.

There is a time to warn and a time to encourage, and the Instructor knows his congregation needed more encouragement and affirmation, yet not without reworking his warning theme. What they needed most was to continue on the path of long faithfulness, and the next chapter develops that very theme in one of the Bible's most quoted chapters.

QUESTIONS FOR REFLECTION AND APPLICATION

1. What do you notice about the Instructor's pastoral heart and tone in the warning passages?

2. While healthy Christian fellowship is important, what are some signs that a church might be one you need to leave?

3. Do you believe you really belong in the house of God? If you struggle with that, how can the Instructor's affirmations assure you of your belonging today?

4. Have you ever been tempted toward apostasy, or have you ever been afraid of apostasy?

5. What did your faith look like when it was most vibrant? Is that your experience right now, or are you experiencing a dimming of your faith life?

THE SON AND FAITH: FROM CREATION TO JOSEPH

Hebrews 11:1–22

¹ Now faith is confidence in what we hope for and assurance about what we do not see. ² This is what the ancients were commended for.

³ By faith we understand that the universe was formed at God's command, so that what is seen was not made out of what was visible.

⁴ By faith Abel brought God a better offering than Cain did. By faith he was commended as righteous, when God spoke well of his offerings. And by faith Abel still speaks, even though he is dead.

⁵ By faith Enoch was taken from this life, so that he did not experience death: "He could not be found, because God had taken him away." For before he was taken, he was commended as one who pleased God. ⁶ And without faith it is impossible to please God, because anyone who comes to him must believe that he exists and that he rewards those who earnestly seek him.

⁷ By faith Noah, when warned about things not yet seen, in holy fear built an ark to save his family. By his faith he condemned the world and became heir of the righteousness that is in keeping with faith.

⁸ *By faith Abraham, when called to go to a place he would later receive as his inheritance, obeyed and went, even though he did not know where he was going. ⁹ By faith he made his home in the promised land like a stranger in a foreign country; he lived in tents, as did Isaac and Jacob, who were heirs with him of the same promise. ¹⁰ For he was looking forward to the city with foundations, whose architect and builder is God. ¹¹ And by faith even Sarah, who was past childbearing age, was enabled to bear children because she considered him faithful who had made the promise. ¹² And so from this one man, and he as good as dead, came descendants as numerous as the stars in the sky and as countless as the sand on the seashore.*

¹³ *All these people were still living by faith when they died. They did not receive the things promised; they only saw them and welcomed them from a distance, admitting that they were foreigners and strangers on earth. ¹⁴ People who say such things show that they are looking for a country of their own. ¹⁵ If they had been thinking of the country they had left, they would have had opportunity to return. ¹⁶ Instead, they were longing for a better country—a heavenly one. Therefore God is not ashamed to be called their God, for he has prepared a city for them.*

¹⁷ *By faith Abraham, when God tested him, offered Isaac as a sacrifice. He who had embraced the promises was about to sacrifice his one and only son, ¹⁸ even though God had said to him, "It is through Isaac that your offspring will be reckoned." ¹⁹ Abraham reasoned that God could even raise the dead, and so in a manner of speaking he did receive Isaac back from death.*

²⁰ *By faith Isaac blessed Jacob and Esau in regard to their future.*

²¹ *By faith Jacob, when he was dying, blessed each of Joseph's sons, and worshiped as he leaned on the top of his staff.*

²² *By faith Joseph, when his end was near, spoke about the exodus of the Israelites from Egypt and gave instructions concerning the burial of his bones.*

From the outset of this letter, the Instructor has pressed the audience toward understanding that genuine faith is a long faithfulness (cf. 4:2; 6:1, 12; 10:22), which means a faith that is both (1) not perfect or sinless but that is (2) a lifetime of trust. In our tidy world we'd like to have had some clear definitions. I know I would have liked an early, straight-up statement of what the sin in those warning passages actually is, and in calling us to a long faithfulness, for which the author uses an abundance of terms, I would have liked a clarifying word. We get a definition and more in today's reading, which twins with the next day's reading. Chapter eleven of Hebrews defines the "faith" of long faithfulness.

We are perhaps tempted to think of the roll call of the faithful in today's reading as a list of champions, of winners, of those who had it all and did it all. But that's just not true. Each of the persons in this list failed, and if their failures are not mentioned, we know they failed because we know the top person here, Abraham, flopped a few times himself, and so did Moses. I like the words in a sermon preached in Duke's chapel by Leander Keck: The Instructor "has no word for Christian winters. But he does have a word for those of us whose bright summer of religious experience may be fading, who sense that the fizz has gone out of life, and who need a sense of direction grounded in reality. Our text has a word for everyone who is threatened by despair because life is falling short of the glamorized success portrayed in the ads" (Keck, "Seeing and Not Seeing," 212). *Yes*, I would say, again I would say *yes*. Faith is for the long journey, and all long journeys know the experiences of getting lost, of wondering where we are, and of being all tuckered out.

FAITH DEFINED

Speaking of definitions, the Instructor defines faith in 11:1, and I will provide three translations of that verse:

"Now faith is confidence in what we hope for and assurance about what we do not see." (NIV)

"Now faith is the assurance of things hoped for, the conviction of things not seen." (NRSVue)

"Faith is the reality of what we hope for, the proof of what we don't see." (CEB)

Definitions help, as long as you understand the terms used in the definition. Hebrews 11:1 has some tricky terms in its definition. One term is especially difficult. The Greek term *hypostasis* is translated variously in the translations above: *confidence, assurance, reality*. A second term, *elenchos*, is not as difficult but still leads to various translations: *assurance, conviction, proof*.

My *Cambridge Greek Lexicon* uses the following terms for the first word: "that which forms a foundation or basis, **groundwork**," and then offers a second set of terms: "capacity to put up resistance, **endurance, steadfastness**" (Diggle, *Cambridge*, 1439, bold font original). The first set of terms describe how it is used in a narrative or for a building, and the second for people. We can be reasonably confident that term expresses faith as the most genuine reality of all and thus the foundation for following Jesus over the long haul, while the second set of terms helps too. Faith endures. All along I have used "long faithfulness" because of how faith is defined in 11:1.

That same lexicon defines the second term, *elenchus*, with the following glosses: "technique of argument for the purpose of disproof or refutation; **refutation**," and adds that it could have the sense of "**examination, investigation**" and also of "**evidence, proof**" (Diggle, *Cambridge*, 466, bold font original). When we add "about what we do not see" to *elenchus*, we land firmly on the side of the NRSVue above ("the conviction of things not seen"). The NIV's "assurance" then naturally flows out of one's conviction that what God promised will occur. David deSilva helpfully offers the sense that *elenchus* is "a *living witness to a greater reality*" (deSilva, *Hebrews*, 103). A long faithfulness lives out of the conviction that God's promise is good because God is trustworthy. Faith, which in this sense is "allegiance" (*Second Testament*), is not a one-and-done moment but a lifetime of moments of trusting God and God's promises.

Definitions are guideposts but the examples of people living out a long faithfulness provide the embodied realities of faith, the faith for which they were "commended" (11:2). The Greek term behind "commended" is often translated with "witness" or "testify," the very term the Instructor will use to sum up the individuals of chapter eleven at 12:2 as a "great cloud of witnesses." Hence, the sense is that these elders or ancients witness to the faith defined by the Instructor.

FAITH DISPLAYED

Throughout these examples of faith displayed, we constantly encounter faith as *living obediently today based upon trusting God and in God's promised future*, and we don't even need to be reminded that the future is the Rest, or final entrance into the fullness of God's presence in the kingdom of God. The present life of faith lives into God's future (cf. 10:23, 36, 38). We are not to reduce faith to believing facts about God or salvation. Faith is an interpersonal relationship of ongoing trust, and hence faith and love are integrally related in the Bible. Which means faith is trusting God because of *who* God is and *what* God can and will do.

These examples of faith shape our imaginations toward:

> Pilgrims caught between past and future in a very demanding present, and their trust in God's concern for them gave them perspective, patience, and persistence. All were persons of their time, but stirred by the forward look; they were seekers, impelled by what was yet to be, encouraged by what they anticipated. They all sensed that the meaning of their days would be clarified in time and vindicated by God." (Massey-Kaalund, "Hebrews," 484)

The term *pilgrim* perfectly captures faith as a journey of long faithfulness. Faith is not for the day visitor; faith is for the pilgrim. Faith is a life shaped by God's future.

WE

In today's reading, the faith of one group and seven individuals is used to exemplify the long faithfulness the Instructor has in mind. It begins with the group, with "we," and that means the Instructor and his people (11:3). "By faith **we** understand" and affirm and live in light of the fact of God speaking the world into existence. We need to hover over another term. The word "universe" translates *aiōn*, which has every bit of a sense of time as it does of the material world. So, "universe" needs to be understood as this world shaped by a history, a present, and a future. The term conveys time as a sequence of ages or eras. Amy Peeler gets it exactly right in translating it with "times, spaces, and the things that fill them" (Peeler, *Hebrews*, 312).

God created what we see out of what we cannot see.

Genesis 1:1's terms are that what existed, or what did not exist, was "formless and empty" (Hebrew *tohu va-bohu*) and swarmed by "darkness" with the "Spirit of God hovering over the waters." The Instructor is interpreting Genesis 1:1 as turning chaos and nothingness into orderly and time-shaped something-ness. The Instructor's emphasis is that all creation owes its origins and existence to God; the emphasis is not on the *how* or the *process* of creation but on God who is the Creator. This example is the only one that does not base living now in light of the future. Instead, this one bases life now on the past origins of all creation, or more precisely, on the Creator.

We will not encounter a collective again until the Instructor interrupts his Abraham story with an "all these people" synthesis (11:13–16), which is then followed by more about Abraham. A final collective summary will be found at the end of the chapter (11:39–40), who will become the Instructor's "great cloud of witness" (12:1).

People of Faith in the Old Testament	
Abel	Genesis 4:1–16
Enoch	Genesis 5:21–24
Noah	Genesis 6–9
Abraham	Genesis 11:27–25:11
Sarah	Genesis 17–18, 20–21, 23
Isaac	Genesis 17, 21–22, 24–28
Jacob	Genesis 25, 27–37, 42, 45–49
Joseph	Genesis 30, 33, 35, 37, 39–50
Moses	Exodus
Jericho	Joshua 6
Rahab	Joshua 2

ABEL, ENOCH, AND NOAH

We can keep in mind what faith is: *living obediently today based upon trusting God and in God's promised future.* Without our knowing that he had been instructed by God about what to sacrifice, Abel presented to God a more acceptable "offering" than the one offered by Cain, his brother (Genesis 4:1–16). His faith, like Abraham's would be, led to God's affirmation that he was "righteous"—that is, that he had done God's will (Hebrews 11:4). The Instructor turns Abel into an example of doing God's will as instructed by God with "Abel still speaks."

Enoch, like Elijah, did not die but was "taken from this life" (11:5), and the rapture of Enoch witnessed to God's affirmation of his life of a long faithfulness (300 years! Genesis 5:21–24). Enoch's story gives the Instructor an opportunity to fill in his definition of faith (Hebrews 11:1), which brings out both the necessity of the reality of God (11:3) and the need to live toward divine approval: "without faith it is impossible to please God, because anyone who comes to him must believe that he exists and that he rewards those who earnestly seek him" (11:6).

Noah, surrounded by corruption, chose to live before God and for God's future. So, he famously built the ark and, in so doing, turned his back on the "world" and became the "heir of righteousness." By the way, the Instructor does not mention "Noah's crashed ark on Mount Ararat," which would support the theme that not everything goes smoothly for those doing God's will (Singleton, *Asides*, 77). Righteousness is behavior that conforms to God's will, and such obedience corresponds with a faithfulness that is long (11:7).

A witness to the life of faith illustrates the Instructor's roll call of the faithful: "The more time I spend in God's presence, in prayer, and in listening to God, the more the divine reality impresses itself upon me, the perspective of faith is restored, and the directions in which faith leads becomes evident" (deSilva, *Hebrews*, 105).

Faith Is . . .

Faith is the willingness to trust our lives and our future to God, even when God does not appear to be as reliable as other, more immediate supports. Faith is readiness to risk life on the promises of God without holding back. (Brueggemann, *Collected Sermons*, 206)

They believed they were on the right trail, for they had seen no other. (Willa Cather, *Death Comes for the Archbishop*, 65)

And here is the key: [the examples of faith] not seeing it happen in history is not their personal tragedy. Rather, their not seeing their dreams fulfilled is a sign that their vision embraced what is noble, enduring, and transcendent. In pursuing it, they were themselves made noble, strong as oaks, and effective in ways they could not see. Because they achieve less than they sought, they actually achieved more. (Keck, "Seeing and Not Seeing," 216)

Faith is only faith in deeds of obedience. (Bonhoeffer, *Discipleship*, 64)

While it may seem more respectable to approach faith as an intellectual exercise or more satisfying to approach it as an emotional one, our relationship to God is not simply a matter of what we think or how we feel. It is more comprehensive than that, and more profound. It is a full-bodied relationship in which mind and heart, spirit and flesh, are converted to a new way of experiencing and responding to the world. It is the surrender of one set of images and the acceptance of another. It is a matter of learning to see the world, each other, and ourselves as God sees us, and to live as if God's reality were the only one that mattered. (Barbara Brown Taylor, *Preaching Life*, 44)

Faith deals with all of the reality that rides in upon us. The aim of faith is to *refine* life where it is coarse, to *soften* it where it is hard, to *reconcile* it where it is lost, to *value* it where it is debased, to *celebrate* it where it is doubted, to *free* it where it is hung up, and to *illuminate* where it is in darkness. (Ernest Campbell, "What's the Story?" 171; his italics)

To believe that is an act of faith, which is an imaginative act. In faith, we imagine ourselves whole, imagine ourselves in love with our neighbors, imagine ourselves bathed and fed by God, imagine the creation at peace, imagine the breath of God coinciding with our own, imagine the heart of God beating at the heart of the world. It is a vision of the kingdom, but is it true or false, fact or fiction? That is the question God continues to ask us: What is real to us, what is true, and what do we intend to do about it? (Barbara Brown Taylor, *Preaching Life*, 53)

ABRAHAM AND SARAH

Abraham is for Christians exactly what he was for Israel and for Judaism: the man who best exhibited faith as a long faithfulness (Genesis 11:27–25:11). Notice the action words connected to Abraham's faith: "when called . . . [he] obeyed and went"; he "made his home in the promised land like a stranger"; "he lived in tents" (Hebrews 11:8–9). Faith actions lead the Instructor to another extrapolation about faith, this time with Abraham showing that a long faithfulness lives in the present in light of God's future, "the city with foundations, whose architect and builder is God" (11:10).

Most translations encompass the Sarah story in her husband's story, but her story deserves to be given proper notice (11:11–12; Isaiah 51:2 does). She was "enabled" by God's redemptive act to "bear children" because she, too, trusted God's promise for future children. Her descendants, we are reminded, were and are "as numerous" as stars and grains of sand (Hebrews 11:12). Both Abraham and Sarah believed God's promise and lived faithfully into God's future, with bumps and bruises along the way.

Themes of Faith in Hebrews 11

1. Faith acts with a view to the unseen.
2. Faith acts with a view to the future.
3. Faith invests in eternal goods.
4. Faith acts in the confident hope of the Resurrection.
5. Living by faith brings lasting honor.

—David deSilva, *Hebrews*, 103–111.

Pastoral Moment

The Instructor interrupts the Abraham-Sarah story of faith with a commentary about faith (11:13–16). "All these people" exemplify the Instructor's understanding of faith as long faithfulness. Remember what faith is: *living obediently today based upon trusting God and in God's promised future.* We see this in the Instructor's commentary: In 11:13 we read that they died while still believing; they knew God's future was still in the future; they saw themselves as non-residents of a worldly existence. This future orientation of faith turns on knowing there is a "better country," namely "a heavenly one" (11:14–16). And a life of faithfulness that keeps its eyes on the final Rest is one that is approved by the God who "has prepared a city for them" (11:16). In this brief commentary on faith, the Instructor draws out "God's promised future" as shaping a life of faith in the present.

Abraham, Isaac, Jacob, and Joseph

The famous *Aqedah*, or (near) sacrifice of Isaac by Abraham (Genesis 22), becomes a separable illustration of a long faithfulness (Hebrews 11:17–19). The tension in the story was always present, and the Instructor brings it to the fore: To Abraham was promised a son and descendants, but offering him would undo that line. The Instructor reads into the Genesis story that Abraham's perception of God's future for him could involve resurrection (11:19).

Each of Abraham's descendants manifested long faithfulness because their present was determined by God's future, with their own incidents of failures. Isaac "blessed" his sons for their future; Jacob blessed Joseph's son for their future;

and Joseph anticipated God's ransom and liberation of the children of Israel from Egypt.

A Modern Exhortation

I don't know about you, but reading Hebrews 11's exhibitions of faith encourages me to carry on in my own attempts to follow Jesus. However, they discourage me about how faith has become, among far too many, little more than a singular act in one moment of time. That is, for many "to believe" or to accept in "faith" the gospel happened once in the past. The Instructor will have none of that. Faith for him, as this chapter shows and as the next day's reading will show, is continuing faith and ongoing trust. The affirmation of God is for a faith characterized as long faithfulness. It is a faith that lives for entry into the promised Rest, the kingdom of God, that final and eternal entry into the very presence of God. Our evangelism needs to be tied to courses on discipleship, and that means the first act of faith needs to be emphasized as the first in a life of acts that make up a long faithfulness. For many, this might seem radical. For such persons, I exhort them to read Hebrews until this vision of long faithfulness takes root.

Questions for Reflection and Application

1. How does the Instructor define faith?

2. How does McKnight define faith?

3. Based on these examples, it is clear that life does not always go well for people who live by faith. How do their life stories impact your understanding of a life of faith?

4. Why is discipleship an essential counterpart to evangelism?

5. How does keeping our eyes on the future Rest and future reality help us live in faithfulness today?

FOR FURTHER READING

Dietrich Bonhoeffer, *Discipleship* (Minneapolis: Fortress, 2001).

Walter Brueggemann, *The Collected Sermons of Walter Brueggemann* (Philadelphia: Westminster John Knox, 2011).

Ernest T. Campbell, "What's the Story?," in W. Willimon, ed., *Sermons from Duke Chapel: Voices from "A Great Towering Church"* (Durham: Duke University Press, 2005), 166–171.

Willa Cather, *Death Comes for the Archbishop*, Everyman's Library (New York: A. A. Knopf, 1992).

J. Diggle, editor in chief, *The Cambridge Greek Lexicon*, 2 vols. (Cambridge: Cambridge University Press, 2021). The lexicon uses bold font as translations of the Greek terms.

Leander Keck, "Seeing and Not Seeing," in W. Willimon, ed., *Sermons from Duke Chapel: Voices from "A Great Towering Church"* (Durham: Duke University Press, 2005), 211–217.

George Singleton, *Asides: Occasional Essays* (Rochester, Massachusetts: Eastover, 2023).

Barbara Brown Taylor, *The Preaching Life* (Boston: Cowley, 1993).

THE SON AND FAITH: FROM MOSES TO THE PRESENT

Hebrews 11:23–12:3

23 By faith Moses' parents hid him for three months after he was born, because they saw he was no ordinary child, and they were not afraid of the king's edict.

24 By faith Moses, when he had grown up, refused to be known as the son of Pharaoh's daughter. 25 He chose to be mistreated along with the people of God rather than to enjoy the fleeting pleasures of sin. 26 He regarded disgrace for the sake of Christ as of greater value than the treasures of Egypt, because he was looking ahead to his reward. 27 By faith he left Egypt, not fearing the king's anger; he persevered because he saw him who is invisible. 28 By faith he kept the Passover and the application of blood, so that the destroyer of the firstborn would not touch the firstborn of Israel.

29 By faith the people passed through the Red Sea as on dry land; but when the Egyptians tried to do so, they were drowned.

30 By faith the walls of Jericho fell, after the army had marched around them for seven days.

31 By faith the prostitute Rahab, because she welcomed the spies, was not killed with those who were disobedient.

³² And what more shall I say? I do not have time to tell about Gideon, Barak, Samson and Jephthah, about David and Samuel and the prophets, ³³ who through faith conquered kingdoms, administered justice, and gained what was promised; who shut the mouths of lions, ³⁴ quenched the fury of the flames, and escaped the edge of the sword; whose weakness was turned to strength; and who became powerful in battle and routed foreign armies. ³⁵ Women received back their dead, raised to life again. There were others who were tortured, refusing to be released so that they might gain an even better resurrection. ³⁶ Some faced jeers and flogging, and even chains and imprisonment. ³⁷ They were put to death by stoning; they were sawed in two; they were killed by the sword. They went about in sheepskins and goatskins, destitute, persecuted and mistreated—³⁸ the world was not worthy of them. They wandered in deserts and mountains, living in caves and in holes in the ground.

³⁹ These were all commended for their faith, yet none of them received what had been promised, ⁴⁰ since God had planned something better for us so that only together with us would they be made perfect.

^{12:1} Therefore, since we are surrounded by such a great cloud of witnesses, let us throw off everything that hinders and the sin that so easily entangles. And let us run with perseverance the race marked out for us, ² fixing our eyes on Jesus, the pioneer and perfecter of faith. For the joy set before him he endured the cross, scorning its shame, and sat down at the right hand of the throne of God. ³ Consider him who endured such opposition from sinners, so that you will not grow weary and lose heart.

I was biting my tongue the whole time we were going through the previous passage (11:1–22). I wanted so much to jump ahead, not only to today's reading, but all the way to the end of today's reading. That is, to 12:1–3, which explains best how to read 11:1–39. Let me explain what I have now stated. If you cut out the warning passages of Hebrews (see Appendix) you will see a list of topics, each of which revolves around the Son and *someone or something.* The Son and Angels, the Son and Moses, and then the Son and the High Priest, which opens up several sub-topics about the Son and the temple system of redemption: the Son and Melchizedek, the Son and Covenant, the Son and Tabernacle, and the Son and Sacrifice. Then we get a long passage about Faith. We then must ask, "How does the faith chapter fit with the Instructor's pattern of 'The Son and . . . ?'" Here's how: Hebrews 12:1–3 shows us that the long faithfulness from Creation to the Martyrs becomes possible *only by keeping our eyes fixed on Jesus.* His faith was better than the faith of all those listed in chapter eleven. In fact, their faith draws its powers from his faith, even if his faithfulness was in their future!

So, we can say that faith in 11:1–12:3 is the last of the theological topics in the book of Hebrews, and it can be labeled the "Son and Faith." Hebrews 11 is not a warning passage. But neither is it simply a theoretical discussion about faith. Rather, because the completion of chapter eleven is not until 12:1–3, Hebrews 11 is like all the other theological topics in Hebrews. It is about the Son and Faith. The Instructor does not finish off Hebrews 11:1–38 with "Now follow their example." That he doesn't is both noticeable and suggestive for us to read beyond the English Bible chapter division into the beginning of chapter twelve. So, instead of "Follow their example," the Instructor says, "Look to Jesus."

LOOKING TO JESUS

Recall that long faithfulness is *living obediently today based upon trusting God and in God's promised future.* Notice how *futuristic* long faithfulness of Jesus is: "For the joy set before him he endured the cross, scorning its shame, and sat down at the right hand of the throne of God" (12:2). Those described with faith in the previous reading oriented their daily life toward the promise of God for the future. Jesus, too. In living a life of faithfulness, Jesus became the "pioneer" for those who would follow in his steps, and as the one who finished his calling, he became perfect and the "perfecter of faith" (12:2). In his life he faced "opposition from sinners." He is, therefore, more than an example, more than an illustration. He cut through the thicket and paved the way for you and for me to follow. He is the "Originator" of faithfulness (*Second Testament*). The Instructor hereby suggests that even Abraham and those who followed him were empowered to live faithfully because, like Jesus, they set their eyes on God's promised future.

We are to look to Jesus as those who are "surrounded by such a great cloud of witnesses" (12:1) who were detailed in 11:3–38. In looking to Jesus, we are to shed anything and everything that impedes our long faithfulness. With a lighter load, the Instructor exhorts believers to "run with perseverance," which is yet another expression for long faithfulness (12:1). But the long walk becomes now a race to the finish! Running with perseverance is the life lived by not only Abel to Joseph but also the life from Moses to the Martyrs (11:23–38).

Long Faithfulness

Long faithfulness is
living obediently
today
based upon trusting God and in God's promised future.

WITH MEMORIES OF
OUR FORBEARS

If we look first to Jesus, we will see those who have journeyed on the path of a long faithfulness. The Instructor's long chapter about faith reveals that he wants us to know about our forebears in the faith. Yet, he will say that only when the fullness of time is complete will a long faithfulness meet its final Rest and reward (11:39–40). It will be good for us to pause here to ponder those who have come before us in the faith, those who taught us the faith but who also showed us the faith.

I think of my father's mother and father, Mildred and Alexander.

Of my father and mother, Alex and Lois.

Of my youth pastors, George Stiekes and David King.

Of a professor who shaped my calling, Joe Crawford.

Of my seminary professors, Murray Harris and Grant Osborne.

Of my doctoral mentor, James D. G. Dunn.

And most of all of my wife, Kris, alongside whom I have walked in faith since the revival of our faith together in the summer of 1971.

I could go on, and I have avoided the many books and friends and students who have shaped my faith, but I turn this now over to you.

We can easily get lost in a history that does not encourage us, that shapes us to a life lived only for this world, that captures our minds and imaginations. Hebrews 11 provides for each of us an "alternative memory," as Walter Brueggemann summarizes what this chapter does for us. This alternative memory of those who have gone before us reshapes our own history so that it "teems with the names of women and men who have acted differently, at risk, with power." He reminds us that we are far too often "forgetters" (Brueggemann, *Collected Sermons*, 24). Which story do we live in? Is it the story of the self, the family, the nation, the job, or is it the story of Jesus Christ? (Campbell, "What's the Story?" 166–167).

MOSES TO RAHAB

The two major figures in the faith of Israel have always been Abraham and Moses, and that's not discounting David, Josiah, or the prophets. Truth be told, Abraham and Moses form the template for long faithfulness. We looked at Abraham in the last reading, and today's opens with a long section about Moses, but the space devoted to each is about the same. Notice the tidy organization: Both of these fathers in the march of long faithfulness are followed by three examples.

The faith of Moses began with his parents, who "hid him for three months" because they knew he was "no ordinary child" (11:23). The NIV misses in its translation "no ordinary child." The Greek word is *asteios*, and it means "attractive" or "beautiful." Turning again to the *Cambridge Greek Lexicon*, we meet the following translation possibilities for *asteios*: urbane, civilized, smart, refined, clever, appealing, attractive, charming, noble, and fine (Diggle, *Cambridge*, 232). The ancient world correlated one's physical appearance with one's character and potential. It's called *physiognomy*—the ability to know someone by examining the physical body. That's what Moses's parents did: They saw a great future in the appearance of the child.

Moses lived up to his *asteios*, though not always, and not perfectly. Here are the actions of Moses that the Instructor brings to front stage: Moses refused to be identified with the court and treasures of Pharaoh (11:24–26); Moses, like Jesus (12:2–3), walked the path of mistreatment in doing God's will and identifying with the children of Israel. In light of the Instructor's understanding of faith, he sums up Moses's long faithfulness as "he regarded disgrace for the sake of Christ as of greater value than the treasures of Egypt, because he was looking ahead to his reward" (11:26). So, he "left Egypt" with the children of Israel, knowing what would happen but not fearing the Pharaoh's wrath or might. Again, reworking his definition, the Instructor says Moses "persevered because he saw him who is invisible" (11:27). A singular action displaying Moses's faith was that he "kept the Passover" that protected and preserved the people of God, and that act was as much an act of faith as it was an act of resistance of Pharaoh (11:28).

As the Instructor followed Abraham with brief examples, so he does the same following Moses (11:29–31), this time turning to (1) the faithful ways of the people choosing to follow Moses through the Red Sea; (2) the willingness for those who passed through the Jordan River to march around Jericho as actions that displayed their trust in God's future victory; and (3) the courage of Rahab, labeled here as a "prostitute," to welcome the spies. Each of these lived that day in light of God's promised future. Along with Sarah (11:11), Rahab shows that faith is exercised by women as well. Surely we are to include women in "the people" who "passed through the Red Sea" (11:29).

GIDEON TO THE MARTYRS

The Instructor's time is running out: "I do not have time" at 11:32 indicates speech more than what is permitted on a sheet of papyrus. He knows he's got a bundle of more stories to tell. But, like the preacher who suddenly realizes he has only a few minutes to get through several important considerations, he chooses to sketch out dozens of stories by mentioning names, beginning with Gideon and including some wild cards, like Barak and Jephthah (see sidebar: "Amy Peeler on Jephthah," 11:32 below), who reaped the rewards of faithfulness in political and social skill, in escaping death, and in military victories (11:33–35a; Cockerill, *Yesterday*, 131–132). Some also suffered much (11:35b–37). Notice these expressions of living each day in light of God's promise, and I will mention only two: "and gained what was promised" (11:33) and "an even better resurrection" (11:35). The Instructor's evaluation echoes loudly even to this day when we think of martyrs for the faith: "The world was not worthy of them" (11:38). Injustice, he hints, will meet its match in God's final justice.

Amy Peeler on Jephthah

Jephthah shares a connection with Rahab; he is the son of a prostitute (Judg 11:1), and his half brothers drive him out. Later his people returned to him to ask him to be their leader, making his rise to power fit the pattern of an unlikely ruler. He has a good memory of Israel's history, recounting events from the time of the wilderness generation and God's provision for them (Judg 11:14–27). His story ends, however, tragically. He defeats the sons of Ammon but in so doing makes a rash vow that results in the death of his daughter (Judg 11:29–40). Then he engages in a battle with fellow Israelites, the tribe of Ephraim, in which thousands die (Judg

> 12:1–7). Jephthah had moments of faith but also moments of infuriating and heartbreaking foolishness, which brought about the death of his own kin. (Peeler, *Hebrews*, 348)
>
> As such, Jephthah, to be as generous as I can be, illustrates the ups and downs of a long faithfulness.

Seemingly countering that brief mention of gaining what was promised (11:33), the Instructor makes it abundantly clear that "none" of these people of faith "received what had been promised" (11:39). Yet they were commended (11:2, 39). Again, what was promised by God was that final Rest, or the kingdom, or that better resurrection, or that city God prepared for them. God's patience lasted beyond those generations of long faithfulness into the present generation. "God had planned something better for us" echoes some of my favorite verses in 1 Peter (1:10–12). God had a plan for Israel, and he has one planned for the people of the Messiah who expand Israel to include gentiles who follow Jesus (Hebrews 11:40). Only when those people of faith are united with the faithful followers of Jesus will "they be made perfect" (11:40).

Walter Brueggemann turns the faith vision of the Instructor into words for us today in what follows, and I urge you to read his words slowly:

> The missional journey is "by faith." By faith is genuinely subversive of all our ideologies. By faith is more radical than all our pet postures. By faith is the edge of God's reality. By faith is a decision for glad, joyous, healing obedience. . . . We are, by faith, a very different people,

sent by God and traveling with God on the journey which is our life." (Brueggemann, *Collected Sermons*, 28)

"By faith," then, is the Instructor's code word for the pilgrim's journey of long faithfulness.

Faith in Hebrews 11 is a backward and forward looking way of life. Amy Peeler says this so well, and I love how she puts it all into poetic lines: "Faith looks back to what God has done and finds the mighty God trustworthy. Faith looks forward to what God has promised to do: defeat the power of death and gather all people who trust in the living Son in resurrected bodies to live forever in the heavenly city, which is the center of renewal for the good creation. This is the faith that unites humanity through all generations. This is the faith that allows endurance and righteous action through whatever difficulties any members of this family may face" (Peeler, *Hebrews*, 358). Amen.

QUESTIONS FOR REFLECTION AND APPLICATION

1. Why do you think the Instructor finishes this faith section by commending the audience to look to Jesus instead of looking to these examples of human faith?

2. What do you learn about the faith of Moses in this reading?

3. Of all the examples of biblical faith in the last two readings, which stands out the most to you, and why?

4. The people of faith mentioned in today's reading, as well as in yesterday's, did not "receive what had been promised." How can their example of faith without tangible payoff encourage you today?

5. Who has taught you how to live a long faithfulness?

FOR FURTHER READING

Walter Brueggemann, *The Collected Sermons of Walter Brueggemann* (Philadelphia: Westminster John Knox, 2011).

Ernest T. Campbell, "What's the Story?," in W. Willimon, ed., *Sermons from Duke Chapel: Voices from "A Great Towering Church"* (Durham: Duke University Press, 2005), 166–171.

J. Diggle, editor in chief, *The Cambridge Greek Lexicon*, 2 vols. (Cambridge: Cambridge University Press, 2021).

AN EXHORTATION TO LONG FAITHFULNESS #5

Hebrews 12:4–29

[4] *In your struggle against sin, you have not yet resisted to the point of shedding your blood.*

[5] *And have you completely forgotten this word of encouragement that addresses you as a father addresses his son? It says,*

> *"My son, do not make light of the Lord's discipline,*
> *and do not lose heart when he rebukes you,*
> [6] *because the Lord disciplines the one he loves,*
> *and he chastens everyone he accepts as his son."*

[7] *Endure hardship as discipline; God is treating you as his children. For what children are not disciplined by their father?* [8] *If you are not disciplined—and everyone undergoes discipline—then you are not legitimate, not true sons and daughters at all.* [9] *Moreover, we have all had human fathers who disciplined us and we respected them for it. How much more should we submit to the Father of spirits and live!* [10] *They disciplined us for a little while as they thought best; but God disciplines us for our good, in order that we may share*

in his holiness. [11] *No discipline seems pleasant at the time, but painful. Later on, however, it produces a harvest of righteousness and peace for those who have been trained by it.*

[12] *Therefore, strengthen your feeble arms and weak knees.* [13] *"Make level paths for your feet," so that the lame may not be disabled, but rather healed.*

[14] *Make every effort to live in peace with everyone and to be holy; without holiness no one will see the Lord.* [15] *See to it that no one falls short of the grace of God and that no bitter root grows up to cause trouble and defile many.* [16] *See that no one is sexually immoral, or is godless like Esau, who for a single meal sold his inheritance rights as the oldest son.* [17] *Afterward, as you know, when he wanted to inherit this blessing, he was rejected. Even though he sought the blessing with tears, he could not change what he had done.*

[18] *You have not come to a mountain that can be touched and that is burning with fire; to darkness, gloom and storm;* [19] *to a trumpet blast or to such a voice speaking words that those who heard it begged that no further word be spoken to them,* [20] *because they could not bear what was commanded: "If even an animal touches the mountain, it must be stoned to death."* [21] *The sight was so terrifying that Moses said, "I am trembling with fear."*

[22] *But you have come to Mount Zion, to the city of the living God, the heavenly Jerusalem. You have come to thousands upon thousands of angels in joyful assembly,* [23] *to the church of the firstborn, whose names are written in heaven. You have come to God, the Judge of all, to the spirits of the righteous made perfect,* [24] *to Jesus the mediator of a new covenant, and to the sprinkled blood that speaks a better word than the blood of Abel.*

[25] *See to it that you do not refuse him who speaks. If they did not escape when they refused him who warned them on earth, how much less will we, if we turn away from him who warns us from heaven?* [26] *At that time his voice shook the earth, but now he has promised, "Once more I will shake not only the earth but also the*

heavens." [27] The words "once more" indicate the removing of what can be shaken—that is, created things—so that what cannot be shaken may remain.

[28] Therefore, since we are receiving a kingdom that cannot be shaken, let us be thankful, and so worship God acceptably with reverence and awe, [29] for our "God is a consuming fire."

Five separate times the Instructor shifts his Sermon from comparing with Christ to exhorting the believers to faithfulness and warning them of the consequences of apostasy. Before looking at the final warning in today's reading, let's pause to consider what long faithfulness *is not.*

Long faithfulness is not:

Perfection or perfect Christian living.

Legalism formed around a new set of requirements for the believer.

Sinlessness, neither of one's intentions, of one's motivations, or of one's actions.

Scrupulosity or an obsession with whether one has done enough good.

Nor does long faithfulness look like these:

Constant joy and ebullient happiness.

Perpetual improvement in one's relationship with God.

Constant growth in one's relationships with others.

Unstoppable success in all we do.

Mountaintop experiences each day or each week.

Total satisfaction with one's role at church.

Beautiful relationships with everyone in one's church.

Visible deep commitment to Christ by each Christian we know.

That's what long faithfulness *is not*. Now to what it *is*. Long faithfulness, one more time, is *living obediently today based upon trusting God and in God's promised future*. Long faithfulness is nothing other than daily decisions to follow Jesus as we are empowered by him. Long faithfulness is ordinary loving by ordinary people over time. Long faithfulness entails prayer and Bible reading and worship and fellowship and pursuing justice and peace and wisdom. Long faithfulness is a life lived in the Spirit and thus is a life of learning to love God, to love oneself, and to love others, with Jesus as our sole pioneer and perfecter (Hebrews 2:10; 12:2).

As the Instructor continues to wind down his Sermon, he finishes off his exhortations and warnings by instructing us all how to think better. At times a long faithfulness requires learning to train the mind to think differently. I would want to add that the Instructor was not appealing to the so-called power of positive thinking. Rather, his approach to thinking flowed directly from what believers were to think about God, about God's future, and about living today in relationship with God.

THINK DIVINE EDUCATION

After reminding believers that their "struggle against sin" had not led to the "shedding of blood" (12:4), he turns his eyes toward them and, in a pastoral voice, asks them if they need to think of what they were going through as an opportunity to see God *educating* them as a father educates a son (12:5–6; citing Proverbs 3:11–12). Most translations transcend, properly, the patriarchal father-son theme of Proverbs and thus have "children" instead of "son" (*Second Testament*, NRSVue; CEB has "sons and daughters"; but see NIV at Hebrews 12:5–6's use of "son"). The term he uses is *paideia*, the singularly most important, comprehensive word used for education in the ancient world. So, he urges them to be "resilient" in their divine education (12:7; *Second Testament*). He takes his cue from parenting, and all parents educated their children (12:7–11).

The English term *discipline* has two connotations that do not fit with the Greek term *paideia*, and hence I'm not in favor of translating *paideia* with "discipline." The first is that to discipline someone means to punish them, as when we hear: "That child must be *disciplined.*" The second sense is that it means rigorous self-discipline, like getting up at 4 a.m. every day to run five miles, like not eating until the evening, like working one hour more at the beginning and at the end of the day, like making twenty-five free throws in a row before leaving the gym (I know this experience), or like deciding to pray two hours each day. The term at work in today's reading, while it can have suggestions at times of punishment or self-discipline, has a more general sense of education. The Instructor, in other words, is asking believers to do some self-examination with these questions:

What am I learning from this difficult circumstance?

About God? About God's future?

About what God is calling me to do as I journey with others on the path following Jesus?

How is this challenging experience educating me as a follower of Jesus?

If we see the suffering of the believers in Hebrews as divine punishment, or even God's actions to drive them into rigorous living, we turn God into a monster who is not doing good. Such a God appeals to some, but that is not the God of the Bible. God does not do bad things to make people good. Rather, when we experience bad things—loss of a job, bad news from the doctor, unfortunate collapses in relationships and marriage—we are to trust in God and, in trusting over time, we learn the lessons that come our way by being faithful (2 Corinthians 1 is a good example from Paul's life). That is divine education. As James Massey and Jennifer Kaalund write, "What is painful can be made purposeful, instructive, positive in its issue" (Massey-Kaalund, "Hebrews," 485). Notice "in its issue"; not "in its divine intent." We learn in the pain the disciplines of formation. God's form of education is toward what is beneficial and what leads to sharing in divine holiness (Hebrews 12:10). Education through the challenges of life can be painful in the moment, but down the path of this journey it produces "righteousness," that is, learning to do what is right, just, and peaceful before God (12:11). As David deSilva reminds us, the Instructor "recommends that they view these experiences entirely as training exercises God has placed in front of them to shape them" (deSilva, *Hebrews*, 120).

For the pilgrims on the path of looking straight ahead at Jesus (12:2), the lessons learned through the journey form our character, our behaviors, and our dispositions—and the lessons lead us into the ways of goodness, righteousness, and peace. Those who have gone through the school of divine education are called "wise."

THINK JESUS

Two metaphors for physical education can provide new mental skills for believers. We are "to straighten up [our] dropped hands and [our] paralyzed knees" (12:12, *Second Testament*). The Greek verb used here, *anorthoō*, pictures an action of re-straightening, or restoring, or rebuilding one's disordered hands and arthritic knees. Those of a certain age can relate. I am jerked into life in the morning by a stiff back, I clamber out of my La-Z-Boy chair with stiff knees and ankles, and when I pinch a plastic bag, the arthritis in my fingers sends out a warning signal. Age was not the problem for the believers; faithfulness was. The weakness the Instructor has in mind pertains to the journey, and the routine temptation to abandon the path, to depart from Christian behaviors, and to refuse to listen to God (cf. 12:14–17, 25). The solution is to be restored, to be rebuilt, to straighten up, and so be healed of the weakness (12:13).

We have learned enough from the Instructor to know that he does not think we can do this in our powers. The power to continue the pilgrimage to the Rest comes from God's own work in us, through the Spirit, and by keeping our eyes on the Pioneer and Perfecter of our long faithfulness, Jesus (2:10; 12:2). We need, then, to think clearly about Jesus. Thinking about Jesus has the power to straighten up our wearied bones.

THINK GROUP

This fifth warning, before it gets to the stronger exhortations and warnings (12:25–27), strikes me as more important than we might notice. We all have a tendency—as moderns stuck for good and bad in modernity—to think individualistically. That is, we might be asking ourselves, *How am I doing when it comes to thinking divine about education and thinking about Jesus?* But the Instructor in the heart of this warning passage turns our attention away from ourselves by turning our heads toward the group (12:14–24).

Notice the group-ishness of the Instructor's exhortations, exhortations designed to guide us onward in the journey toward the Rest:

1. They are to "make every effort to live in peace with everyone." (12:14)
2. They are help one another to avoid falling "short of the grace of God." (12:15)
3. They are to make sure no "bitter root" feeds the defilement of "many." (12:15)
4. They are to help one avoid sexual immorality or profaning the community (12:16), and to this the Instructor reminds of the sin of Esau. (12:16–17)

To buttress these group virtues of the community's long faithfulness, the Instructor explores at length the image of approaching two mountains: one that is perceived as untouchable and fiery and destructive (12:18–21) and one that is perceived as gracious, good, and God's (12:22–27). Both mountains are group-ish. The first mountain is Sinai, where God was on the top warning the children of Israel of the consequences of their apostate worshiping of the golden calf. Even Moses feared that mountain (12:21, citing Deuteronomy 9:19; see Exodus 19:12–19).

The second mountain is the City of God. It is "Mount Zion" and the "city of the living God" and the "heavenly Jerusalem," where there are "angels in joyful assembly" and the "church of the firstborn" because this Mountain is "God" and the "spirits of the righteous made perfect" and to "Jesus the mediator of a new covenant" and as well to the "sprinkled blood" of that new covenant (12:22–24). This Mountain, God's Rest and final City, is populated by that "great cloud of witnesses" (12:1) and by those who have journeyed the path of long faithfulness.

Learning to think group takes our eyes off ourselves and our abilities and our gifts and our problems and our sins and relocates them onto Jesus and those who surround him in worship. What helps me in this is to imagine myself at church with others singing a great song that leads us all into our best voices and best feelings as we praise God. When this happens, what happens? We forget ourselves and find God in the center of our thinking. Group worship does that for me, and I suspect it does that for you too (12:14–24).

THINK RESPONSIBILITY

The Instructor's pastoral care leads him several times to instruct and warn his congregation about the importance of being responsible before God. Hebrews 12:25–27 fits with the other warning passages (2:1–4; 3:7–4:13; 5:11–6:12; 10:19–39). The fundamental responsibility in each warning passage is twofold: Don't turn your back on Jesus, and persevere in a long faithfulness (see discussions of the four elements of the warning passages of the passages cited on page 31). There is, after all, a colossal difference between a follower of Jesus and one who does not follow Jesus. Notice, I did not say a "Christian" or a "churchgoer." Those who wander from the path may still want to appear as Christians, and they may be working hard at faking the faith. But there is a difference. The Instructor surely knew that some in his audience were more like the fakes than the faithful.

In this final exhortation his words are these: Run the race (12:1–3) and endure hardship (12:7) and strengthen (12:12) and chase peace (12:14) and see that no one falls from grace or into sexual immorality (12:15, 16), and then at 12:25–27, we get these terms: "Do not refuse him who speaks," with a warning that they will never escape if they do refuse and "turn away from him" (12:25). Then his final exhortations move away from the themes of warning into ordinary faithfulness for ordinary Christians: "Be thankful," or "Let us [or, may we] receive grace" (*Second Testament*), and "Worship God acceptably with reverence and awe" (12:28), bolstering all of this with a reminder from Moses: "For our 'God is a consuming fire,'" which evokes the theme of God as the Jealous One (12:29, citing Deuteronomy 4:24).

The Instructor does not intend to scare people. Some experience his words with fear, however. Rather, the fear of God is connected to the awesomeness of God's omniscience and utter commitment to truth and justice, each of which is shaped by God's love for God's people in God's world. His intent is to remind them of their responsibility to live today with their eyes fixed on Jesus. The Instructor teaches a congregation as a pastor who cares about and for them. He has just made it clear that the mountain they have approached is the God-Mountain of grace, not the fire-mountain of judgment (cf. 12:18 with 12:22). So, his final words in today's reading begin with an important affirmation, which is designed to calm down any inappropriate fears or anxieties about their standing with God: "Since *we* are receiving a kingdom that cannot be shaken . . ." (12:28, emphasis added). That he includes himself reveals that he is confident about their response and their future. He uses a mood that suggests no doubt. He doesn't say "Since we might receive . . ." or "If we do receive . . ." No, his words suggest that he and they are receiving that future kingdom, that Rest. Because that is true, they are to receive grace (or be thankful) and turn to God and worship the God who burns away all sin.

QUESTIONS FOR REFLECTION AND APPLICATION

1. How do the lists of what long faithfulness is and is not help reassure you?

2. What is the role and importance of divine education in our long faithfulness?

3. How can pain and difficulty produce righteousness and wisdom?

4. Which song or songs lead you into the assembly of the faithful?

5. How can you shift your thoughts about the life of long faithfulness from an individual achievement to a corporate experience?

LOVING MATTERS
FOR A LONG
FAITHFULNESS

Hebrews 13:1–25

[1] *Keep on loving one another as brothers and sisters.* [2] *Do not forget to show hospitality to strangers, for by so doing some people have shown hospitality to angels without knowing it.* [3] *Continue to remember those in prison as if you were together with them in prison, and those who are mistreated as if you yourselves were suffering.*

[4] *Marriage should be honored by all, and the marriage bed kept pure, for God will judge the adulterer and all the sexually immoral.*

[5] *Keep your lives free from the love of money and be content with what you have, because God has said,*

> *"Never will I leave you;*
> *never will I forsake you."*

[6] *So we say with confidence,*

> *"The Lord is my helper; I will not be afraid.*
> *What can mere mortals do to me?"*

⁷ *Remember your leaders, who spoke the word of God to you. Consider the outcome of their way of life and imitate their faith. ⁸ Jesus Christ is the same yesterday and today and forever.*

⁹ *Do not be carried away by all kinds of strange teachings. It is good for our hearts to be strengthened by grace, not by eating ceremonial foods, which is of no benefit to those who do so. ¹⁰ We have an altar from which those who minister at the tabernacle have no right to eat.*

¹¹ *The high priest carries the blood of animals into the Most Holy Place as a sin offering, but the bodies are burned outside the camp. ¹² And so Jesus also suffered outside the city gate to make the people holy through his own blood. ¹³ Let us, then, go to him outside the camp, bearing the disgrace he bore. ¹⁴ For here we do not have an enduring city, but we are looking for the city that is to come.*

¹⁵ *Through Jesus, therefore, let us continually offer to God a sacrifice of praise—the fruit of lips that openly profess his name. ¹⁶ And do not forget to do good and to share with others, for with such sacrifices God is pleased.*

¹⁷ *Have confidence in your leaders and submit to their authority, because they keep watch over you as those who must give an account. Do this so that their work will be a joy, not a burden, for that would be of no benefit to you.*

¹⁸ *Pray for us. We are sure that we have a clear conscience and desire to live honorably in every way. ¹⁹ I particularly urge you to pray so that I may be restored to you soon.*

²⁰ *Now may the God of peace, who through the blood of the eternal covenant brought back from the dead our Lord Jesus, that great Shepherd of the sheep, ²¹ equip you with everything good for doing his will, and may he work in us what is pleasing to him, through Jesus Christ, to whom be glory for ever and ever. Amen.*

²² *Brothers and sisters, I urge you to bear with my word of exhortation, for in fact I have written to you quite briefly.*

²³ *I want you to know that our brother Timothy has been released. If he arrives soon, I will come with him to see you.*

²⁴ *Greet all your leaders and all the Lord's people. Those from Italy send you their greetings.*
²⁵ *Grace be with you all.*

How to organize this seemingly random set of instructions before we hear the final *Amen* to this Sermon? James Massey and Jennifer Kaalund observe in passing that the "exhortations [in this last chapter] are all very brief, so brief indeed that it might appear the writer was rushing to complete what had by now become lengthy" (Massey-Kaalund, "Hebrews," 486). Yes, the Instructor quickly gives a number of exhortations, and their connections are not always clear. Yes, his sermon had become lengthy. I suggest we toss a lasso around each of these instructions and pull them into a bundle to view each expressing a dimension of love (see also Pierce, "Hebrews," 605–606). Other letters in the New Testament bundle up final exhortations, encouragements, and items from life at the end too (James 5:12–20; Colossians 4:20–18; 1 Thessalonians 5:12–28). The word *love*, which is one of Paul's favorite terms, makes only two appearances in Hebrews, both in citations of the Old Testament (1:9; 12:6), and does not appear in this final chapter. Yet, each item raised by the Instructor to finish off the Sermon illustrates the early Christian understanding of loving God, loving self, and loving others.

LOVING OTHERS

I stated above that Paul's favorite term for love (*agape*) does not appear in this last chapter, but another word for love does appear (13:1): *philadelphia*, which can be translated as does the NIV, with "loving one another as brothers and sisters," or as "mutual affection" (NRSVue), or as "keep loving each other like family" (CEB), or as "sibling-love" (*Second*

Testament). This exhortation to live with one another as siblings immediately turns into loving others who are not family, and I have translated that as "stranger-love" (13:2), which is a literal translation of the Greek term *philoxenia*: love plus stranger or outsider. You can easily notice the connection of verses one and two with the term *philo-* to open these two terms.

Hospitality shaped earliest Christianity in the house churches from Jerusalem to Rome. While the ancient world did have inns, they could be more expensive than early Christian travelers could afford. The more likely explanation for the importance of hospitality in the early churches is that ancient travelers often stayed with family and friends, and friends of family and friends of friends. That the early churches formed a network shaped by a family ethic provides the only reason needed for the emphasis on hospitality. For early Christian travelers, we can complicate the picture. Many sensed they would be unsafe or unwelcomed in an inn, whether in one provided by a city or at one's own expense. Some hostels were little more than brothels. Local synagogues at times had guest rooms, so Christian hospitality was paved by this Jewish practice. The Christian sense of family and religious identity, then, intensified the need for Christian hospitality.

The Instructor adds a note I heard often growing up in support of Christian hospitality, of which my mother was more than fond. Here's how the Instructor puts it: "Some have been hosts to angels without knowing it" (13:2, CEB). The word used, however, approaches hospitality from a surprising angle. I have translated it as "some 'forgot' [their] being hospitable to envoys [or, angels]." The author uses a word connected to forget twice: "Do not forget (*epilanthanō*) to show hospitality" and "some 'forgot'" (*lanthanō*). The surprising element here is that being hospitable just might end up being entertaining a heaven-sent envoy from God, or what we call *angels*.

Loving siblings in the faith and loving travelers turns into loving the imprisoned (13:3). That the first and third act of love appear to be inner-Christian suggests that the travelers are also siblings in the faith. Prisons were not places of final punishment at the time of this Sermon. They were confinements until the court could meet and decide on the case. During that time, the confined person had to meet his or her own needs, and it fell to Christians to become agents of compassion and mercy to those in prison, especially to those imprisoned for their faith, which is the case in 13:3. Empathy and sympathy for the imprisoned are the Instructor's guidance.

There is no reason for us to get legalistic about the inner-Christian dimension of 13:1–3. If a non-believer needs hospitality, Christian graces apply to the situation all the same. And this now immediately places us into our nation's political debates over immigration, over inappropriate and unchristian labels ("illegal aliens"), and over the need for Christians to treat those who want to be in our country the way ancient Israel itself learned to treat those who entered into their communities. Let us begin with the word *hospitality* and see how that might play itself out in our churches and country today. I have a pastor friend whose church's basement was hospitably turned into a shelter for immigrants (Melissa Pillman, link below).

LOVING SPOUSES

Radical commitments to follow Jesus, which occasionally were inspired by a conviction that Jesus was about to return, led to singleness and celibacy as an ideal (see 1 Corinthians 7). The Instructor veers from, or at least complements, that teaching from the apostle Paul's teachings when in Hebrews 13:4 we hear "Marriage should be honored by all." This sounds like a response to those who advocated for celibacy and were perhaps pushing hard for celibacy as the standard. For the marriage bed to be "unstained [by sin]" is a summary expression of the early Christian commitment to follow God's will about fidelity, adultery, perversities, as well as marriage and remarriage (cf. Leviticus 18; Matthew 5:27–32; 1 Corinthians 7).

The prohibitions, however, need not hog our attention and eclipse the opening affirmation to honor marriage, which means to give it overt affirmations. Singleness was never prohibited in the early church, but some took it too far and degraded marriage as a lesser commitment. Our Christian world has flipped that script and made marriage even more central and, frankly, has made celibacy and singleness weird. Our exaggerations need to shorten themselves so we can overtly affirm celibacy and singleness for those so called.

LOVING CONTENTMENT

Greed, more literally "silver-loving" (*Second Testament*), or the accumulation of wealth in order to hoard resources, to gain status in society, or to deflate the resources of others has always been a human temptation. A term sometimes used for this greediness is *mammonolatry*, the worship of money. To acquire more than we need without distributing to others in need, or to do so begrudgingly without that keen sense of gracious generosity, challenged the ethical lives of the earliest Christians. The Instructor guides believers to pursue, or love, contentment with what they have. The words strike us today if we will let them. "'Contentment' is not a core value in capitalist economies. Quite the opposite: it is the lack of contentment that energizes economies by stimulating both the amassing and the spending of capital" (deSilva, *Hebrews*, 132). Notice this: Our economy in the USA works as it does because we lack contentment. No word in this letter, if followed, would impact our society more than the brief words of 13:5.

Financial contentment for those on the journey toward the Rest comes to those who turn their hearts over to God, who once said he would never abandon his people (13:5, citing Deuteronomy 31:6). By this time, we may all need to be reminded again that the Instructor's sense of life as a journey has kept his eye on Deuteronomy, the law for those in the wilderness journey to the promised land. Knowing the God who provided manna and quail for the children of Israel (Exodus 16) is with us gives the Instructor the pastoral word of "confidence" (Hebrews 13:6) that the same God is our "helper." That means "mere mortals" can do nothing to us.

Loving contentment can be a misused piece of guidance. Those who are unemployed, those who feel unemployable, those whose employment yields insufficient funds, and those surrounded by others who have more than enough can be wounded when others urge contentment. We are wise to use this piece of advice when counseling or instructing those who trapped in or tempted by "silver-loving" longings. There is nothing wrong with earning an income. John Wesley once counseled people to earn what we can, save what we can, and give what we can (Wesley, "Use of Money"). That trio of money's companions, when sitting together at the same table, will work into loving contentment.

LOVING LEADERS

The emphasis here on respecting leaders is noteworthy (13:7–8, 17). Not only does this indicate that the Instructor is evidently not their pastor; it indicates a multi-leadership model. "Leaders" translates a widely used, non-specific, and non-technical term. The Instructor doesn't use the terms Paul uses: elder, bishop/overseer, deacon, or pastor. We should keep the term general: It invites us to pray for, which is what "remember" connotes here—those who are in front of us and guiding us on the path of long faithfulness. The "leaders" here evidently are not in specific offices. The term is about their function and influence in our life. We are to observe "their behavior's outcome" and because it is good and toward the Rest, we are to "copy their allegiance" to Christ (13:7, *Second Testament*). But following our leader is not to supplant following the One who is the Pioneer on the path, Jesus: He is the "same yesterday and today and forever" (13:8). True Christian leaders lead us to follow Christ and not to follow them. They guide us into Christlikeness, not leader-likeness. The measure of a leader is how much he or she nurtures Christlikeness.

The Sandwich Structure of Hebrews 13:7–17

Leaders (13:7–8)
    Jesus the Great High Priest (13:9–16)
Leaders (13:17)

Skip down to verse seventeen, where the Instructor picks up leaders again, this time urging the audience to "be persuaded by" (*Second Testament*) or "have confidence in" them. We naturally "yield" (*Second Testament*) to those in whom we are confident. The NIV's choice of "submit" instead of "yield" suggests to most English readers the same term that is used in other submission texts (e.g., Ephesians 5:21, 22). But the Instructor uses a different term than Paul does, preferring *hypeikō*, which suggests yielding, making way, deferring, and stepping aside. The term, then, does not connote hierarchy, as "submit" does, but yielding to the one who knows the path better. Nor does the Instructor use the term "authority," which appears in the NIV. I find this a disturbing interference by the NIV because it shifts the scene from someone ahead of us on the path to someone over us with authority. There is a "follow me, I can see the path" suggestion to the Instructor's choice of words. Their responsibility is to care for those they lead, and they will answer to God for their pastoral care. The Instructor is pragmatic and knows that yielding to leaders who know the path better leads to "joy" for the leader, and we all know that when *momma's happy, everyone's happy* because we also know that when *momma ain't happy, ain't nobody happy*.

A word of warning: Not all leaders are worthy of following, since "leaders can be at best imperfect and at worst predatory. If there is someone in leadership who does not care how he or she will answer to God and, therefore, does not care too much about those under care, that person is not worthy of trust and submission and should be removed." Those are words of a priest-pastor-professor (Peeler, *Hebrews*, 418). The leaders in the mind of the Instructor are neither perfect nor unworthy of following, and that is the state of all good leaders to this day: neither perfect nor unworthy.

LOVING TRUTH

Tucked inside the two short sections about leaders, which reminds me of a Reuben sandwich at Burt's Deli in our village, is a thick section that was stimulated by the Instructor's comment about Jesus being the same forever. For the Instructor, the Jesus he thinks of is the Great High Priest Jesus (13:9–16), which means 13:8's word about the foreverness of Jesus attaches both to the need for leaders to follow Jesus and to the importance of Jesus' pioneering and perfecting work in his priestly redemptive work. Some evidently had diminished the importance of Jesus' priestly role. Perhaps they were allured into pagan temples and their priests. There they were able to consume "ceremonial foods" (13:9). The Instructor urges the believers to love and embrace the truths about Jesus.

So, our author turns his attention to the themes he sketched in chapters four through ten: the fulfillment of the tabernacle in the work of Christ (13:10). In Christ, God has provided an altar (13:10), a Son of God who "suffered outside the city gate to make the people holy through his own blood" (13:12). Attachment to Christ means participating in his disgrace (13:13). These comparisons turn finally to the "coming" city, the heavenly or new Jerusalem (13:14).

With Jesus as the Great High Priest, whose sacrifice fulfills the tabernacle's sacrifices, the Instructor urges them now "continually [to] offer to God a sacrifice *of praise*" (13:15, emphasis added). The Sermon transfers sacrifice from physical animals to spiritual worship and defines this kind of praise as "lips that openly profess his name" (13:15). That will strike the listeners as an appeal to courageous long faithfulness, which evokes in the Instructor yet another exhortation: "Do not forget to do good and to share with others" (13:16). Lest we think he's hopping from one idea to another, we simply turn to the next clause, and we see a clever connection. Generosity is a "sacrifice" with which "God is pleased."

Did Paul Write Hebrews?

Readers familiar with the endings of Paul's letters may think today's reading sounds like Paul. It does, and it is the only time in the entire Sermon that the Instructor sounds like Paul. The author of Hebrews is probably in Italy, though he could be somewhere else and those from Italy with him wish to send their greetings (13:24). That Timothy is with the author sounds like Paul, but we know of no explicit imprisonments of Timothy from the Pauline letters (13:23). Yet some would say otherwise. That is, when Paul wrote Philemon and Philippians, he was in prison, and since Timothy was with him, it is possible he, too, was in prison (Philemon 1; Philippians 1:1; 2:19–23). These two items—in Italy and with Timothy—possibly connect the author and this Sermon with Paul, but the rest of the Sermon and even a few of the themes in chapter thirteen do not sound like Paul (13:5–6, 9–16), and the emphasis on leaders has only slight connections to Paul (13:7–8, 17, 24). I consider Pauline authorship of Hebrews very unlikely.

LOVING INTERCESSION

The Instructor urges the audience now to "pray for us." Perhaps his words remind you as they did me of Michael W. Smith's wonderful song "Pray for Me," a song about people parting and committing to pray for one another (Smith, "Pray for Me"). The Instructor overtly affirms his own conscience about living "honorably" (13:18), but he is especially concerned that they pray that he "may be restored" to them "soon" (13:19). This may suggest he is in prison, but it certainly implies that the distance between them is not of his own choosing.

LOVING COURTESIES

Common courtesies, like personal information about the Instructor's companions and location and plans, ratcheted up with Christian sensibilities, lead the Instructor to speak/write now of a prayer of intercession he has for them (13:20–21), and this prayer has been used time and time again as a benediction at the end of sermons. (It's one I wish we could all hear more often.) Once again, a theme to open his prayer was developed in the Sermon—the theme of the new covenant in Christ (13:20). His prayer for them is that God would "equip" them to live a long faithfulness and so lead to the Rest, where God expresses his good pleasure for them (13:21).

Remarkably for those of us who have ever read the Sermon in one sitting, he contends his "word of exhortation" was but a précis of what he wanted to deliver (13:22)! Timothy, he informs them, has been "released" from prison. Here, he sounds just like Paul: "If he arrives soon, I will come with him to see you" (13:23). He urges the audience to "greet all your leaders" but also "all the Lord's people" (13:24). He sends greeting from those in Italy (13:24), and in very Pauline fashion, prays that "grace" would "be with you all" (13:25).

Amy Peeler opens her discussion of this last chapter with words that connected with me, and perhaps they will with you too: "The beginning and end of this work called Hebrews are rhetorically imbalanced. What began with a bang ends with a whimper" (Peeler, *Hebrews*, 401). The final chapter is an appendix to a long sermon. The appendix turns the Sermon into a letter and openly makes it clear that what was preferred—embodied presence for the Sermon—was not possible, so he wrote out his Sermon and sent it as a letter. There is no substitute for personal presence, and I don't know about you, but I'll take a written Sermon rather than no Sermon.

QUESTIONS FOR REFLECTION AND APPLICATION

1. What was the importance of hospitality for the early church?

2. How could we learn from the early Christians and do a better job affirming both celibacy and marriage?

3. As we reach the end of this study, who do you think might be the author of Hebrews, the Instructor?

4. Where do you need to seek contentment in your long faithfulness?

5. Which Christian leaders in your life have encouraged you to follow Jesus better, not them?

FOR FURTHER READING

Melissa Pillman: https://www.spreaker.com /episode/s4-e2-melissa-pillman-the-church-as-a -sanctuary—57674676.

Michael W. Smith, "Pray for Me," by Wayne Kirkpatrick and Michael W. Smith. Sony/atv Milene Music, Universal Music, Brentwood Benson Songs. Album: *I 2 (Eye)*, Reunion Records, 1988.

John Wesley, "The Use of Money," https://wesley .nnu.edu/john-wesley/the-sermons-of-john -wesley-1872-edition/sermon-50-the-use-of -money/.

APPENDIX: HEBREWS WITHOUT THE WARNING PASSAGES

THE SON-WORD

1:1 In the past God spoke to our ancestors through the prophets at many times and in various ways, ² but in these last days he has spoken to us by his Son, whom he appointed heir of all things, and through whom also he made the universe. ³ The Son is the radiance of God's glory and the exact representation of his being, sustaining all things by his powerful word. After he had provided purification for sins, he sat down at the right hand of the Majesty in heaven. ⁴ So he became as much superior to the angels as the name he has inherited is superior to theirs.

THE SON AND THE ANGELS

1:5 For to which of the angels did God ever say,

> "You are my Son;
>> today I have become your Father"?

Or again,

"I will be his Father,
and he will be my Son"?

1:6 And again, when God brings his firstborn into the world, he says,

"Let all God's angels worship him."

1:7 In speaking of the angels he says,

"He makes his angels spirits,
and his servants flames of fire."

1:8 But about the Son he says,

"Your throne, O God, will last for ever
and ever;
a scepter of justice will be the scepter
of your kingdom.
[9] You have loved righteousness and hated
wickedness;
therefore God, your God, has set you
above your companions
by anointing you with the oil of joy."

1:10 He also says,

"In the beginning, Lord, you laid the
foundations of the earth,
and the heavens are the work of your hands.
[11] They will perish, but you remain;
they will all wear out like a garment.
[12] You will roll them up like a robe;
like a garment they will be changed.

But you remain the same,
and your years will never end."

1:13 To which of the angels did God ever say,

"Sit at my right hand
until I make your enemies
a footstool for your feet"?

1:14 Are not all angels ministering spirits sent to serve those who will inherit salvation?

2:5 It is not to angels that he has subjected the world to come, about which we are speaking.
⁶ But there is a place where someone has testified:

"What is mankind that you are mindful of them,
a son of man that you care for him?
⁷ You made them a little lower than the angels;
you crowned them with glory and honor
⁸ and put everything under their feet."

In putting everything under them, God left nothing that is not subject to them. Yet at present we do not see everything subject to them. ⁹ But we do see Jesus, who was made lower than the angels for a little while, now crowned with glory and honor because he suffered death, so that by the grace of God he might taste death for everyone.

2:10 In bringing many sons and daughters to glory, it was fitting that God, for whom and through whom everything exists, should make the pioneer of their salvation perfect through what he suffered. ¹¹ Both the one who makes people holy and those who are made holy are of the same family. So Jesus is not ashamed to call them brothers and sisters.

[12] He says,

> "I will declare your name to my brothers
>   and sisters;
>   in the assembly I will sing your praises."

2:13 And again,

> "I will put my trust in him."

And again he says,

> "Here am I, and the children God has
>   given me."

2:14 Since the children have flesh and blood, he too shared in their humanity so that by his death he might break the power of him who holds the power of death—that is, the devil—[15] and free those who all their lives were held in slavery by their fear of death. [16] For surely it is not angels he helps, but Abraham's descendants. [17] For this reason he had to be made like them, fully human in every way, in order that he might become a merciful and faithful high priest in service to God, and that he might make atonement for the sins of the people. [18] Because he himself suffered when he was tempted, he is able to help those who are being tempted.

THE SON AND MOSES

3:1 Therefore, holy brothers and sisters, who share in the heavenly calling, fix your thoughts on Jesus, whom we acknowledge as our apostle and high priest. [2] He was faithful to the one who appointed him, just as Moses was faithful in all God's house. ³ Jesus has been found worthy of greater honor than Moses, just as the builder of a house has greater honor than the house itself. ⁴ For every house is built by someone, but God is the builder of everything. ⁵ "Moses was faithful as a servant in all God's house," bearing witness to what would be spoken by God in the future. ⁶ But Christ is faithful as the Son over God's house. And we are his house, if indeed we hold firmly to our confidence and the hope in which we glory.

THE SON AND THE HIGH PRIEST

4:14 Therefore, since we have a great high priest who has ascended into heaven, Jesus the Son of God, let us hold firmly to the faith we profess. ¹⁵ For we do not have a high priest who is unable to empathize with our weaknesses, but we have one who has been tempted in every way, just as we are—yet he did not sin. ¹⁶ Let us then approach God's throne of grace with confidence, so that we may receive mercy and find grace to help us in our time of need.

5:1 Every high priest is selected from among the people and is appointed to represent the people in matters related to God, to offer gifts and sacrifices for sins. ² He is able to deal gently with those who are ignorant and are going astray, since he himself is subject to weakness. ³ This is why he has to offer sacrifices for his own sins, as well as for the sins of the people. ⁴ And no one takes this honor on himself, but he receives it when called by God, just as Aaron was.

5:5 In the same way, Christ did not take on himself the glory of becoming a high priest. But God said to him,

> "You are my Son;
>   today I have become your Father."

5:6 And he says in another place,

> "You are a priest forever,
>   in the order of Melchizedek."

5:7 During the days of Jesus' life on earth, he offered up prayers and petitions with fervent cries and tears to the one who could save him from death, and he was heard because of his reverent submission. [8] Son though he was, he learned obedience from what he suffered [9] and, once made perfect, he became the source of eternal salvation for all who obey him [10] and was designated by God to be high priest in the order of Melchizedek.

THE SON AND MELCHIZEDEK

6:13 When God made his promise to Abraham, since there was no one greater for him to swear by, he swore by himself, [14] saying, "I will surely bless you and give you many descendants." [15] And so after waiting patiently, Abraham received what was promised.

6:16 People swear by someone greater than themselves, and the oath confirms what is said and puts an end to all argument. [17] Because God wanted to make the unchanging nature of his purpose very clear to the heirs of what was promised, he confirmed it with an oath. [18] God did this so that, by two unchangeable things in which it is impossible for God to lie, we who have fled to take hold of the hope set before us may be greatly encouraged. [19] We have this hope as an anchor for the soul, firm and secure. It enters the inner sanctuary behind the curtain, [20] where our forerunner, Jesus, has entered on our behalf. He has become a high priest forever, in the order of Melchizedek.

7:1 This Melchizedek was king of Salem and priest of

God Most High. He met Abraham returning from the defeat of the kings and blessed him, [2] and Abraham gave him a tenth of everything. First, the name Melchizedek means "king of righteousness"; then also, "king of Salem" means "king of peace." [3] Without father or mother, without genealogy, without beginning of days or end of life, resembling the Son of God, he remains a priest forever.

7:4 Just think how great he was: Even the patriarch Abraham gave him a tenth of the plunder! [5] Now the law requires the descendants of Levi who become priests to collect a tenth from the people—that is, from their fellow Israelites—even though they also are descended from Abraham. [6] This man, however, did not trace his descent from Levi, yet he collected a tenth from Abraham and blessed him who had the promises. [7] And without doubt the lesser is blessed by the greater. [8] In the one case, the tenth is collected by people who die; but in the other case, by him who is declared to be living. [9] One might even say that Levi, who collects the tenth, paid the tenth through Abraham, [10] because when Melchizedek met Abraham, Levi was still in the body of his ancestor.

7:11 If perfection could have been attained through the Levitical priesthood—and indeed the law given to the people established that priesthood—why was there still need for another priest to come, one in the order of Melchizedek, not in the order of Aaron? [12] For when the priesthood is changed, the law must be changed also. [13] He of whom these things are said belonged to a different tribe, and no one from that tribe has ever served at the altar. [14] For it is clear that our Lord descended from Judah, and in regard to that tribe Moses said nothing about priests. [15] And what we have said is even more clear if another priest like Melchizedek appears, [16] one who has become a priest not on the basis of a regulation as to his ancestry but on the basis of the power of an indestructible life.

¹⁷ For it is declared:

> "You are a priest forever,
>   in the order of Melchizedek."

7:18 The former regulation is set aside because it was weak and useless ¹⁹ (for the law made nothing perfect), and a better hope is introduced, by which we draw near to God.

7:20 And it was not without an oath! Others became priests without any oath,

²¹ but he became a priest with an oath when God said to him:

> "The Lord has sworn
>   and will not change his mind:
>   'You are a priest forever.'"

7:22 Because of this oath, Jesus has become the guarantor of a better covenant.

7:23 Now there have been many of those priests, since death prevented them from continuing in office; ²⁴ but because Jesus lives forever, he has a permanent priesthood. ²⁵ Therefore he is able to save completely those who come to God through him, because he always lives to intercede for them.

7:26 Such a high priest truly meets our need—one who is holy, blameless, pure, set apart from sinners, exalted above the heavens. ²⁷ Unlike the other high priests, he does not need to offer sacrifices day after day, first for his own sins, and then for the sins of the people. He sacrificed for their sins once for all when he offered himself. ²⁸ For the law appoints as high priests men in all their weakness; but the oath, which came after the law, appointed the Son, who has been made perfect forever.

THE SON AND THE COVENANT

8:1 Now the main point of what we are saying is this: We do have such a high priest, who sat down at the right hand of the throne of the Majesty in heaven, ² and who serves in the sanctuary, the true tabernacle set up by the Lord, not by a mere human being.

8:3 Every high priest is appointed to offer both gifts and sacrifices, and so it was necessary for this one also to have something to offer. ⁴ If he were on earth, he would not be a priest, for there are already priests who offer the gifts prescribed by the law. ⁵ They serve at a sanctuary that is a copy and shadow of what is in heaven. This is why Moses was warned when he was about to build the tabernacle: "See to it that you make everything according to the pattern shown you on the mountain." ⁶ But in fact the ministry Jesus has received is as superior to theirs as the covenant of which he is mediator is superior to the old one, since the new covenant is established on better promises.

8:7 For if there had been nothing wrong with that first covenant, no place would have been sought for another.

⁸ But God found fault with the people and said:

> "The days are coming, declares the Lord,
>   when I will make a new covenant
> with the people of Israel
>   and with the people of Judah.
> ⁹ It will not be like the covenant
>   I made with their ancestors
> when I took them by the hand
>   to lead them out of Egypt,
> because they did not remain faithful to my
>   covenant,
>   and I turned away from them,

declares the Lord.
[10] This is the covenant I will establish with
    the people of Israel
after that time, declares the Lord.
I will put my laws in their minds
    and write them on their hearts.
I will be their God,
    and they will be my people.
[11] No longer will they teach their neighbor,
    or say to one another, 'Know the Lord,'
because they will all know me,
    from the least of them to the greatest.
[12] For I will forgive their wickedness
    and will remember their sins no more."

8:13 By calling this covenant "new," he has made the first one obsolete; and what is obsolete and outdated will soon disappear.

THE SON AND THE TABERNACLE

9:1 Now the first covenant had regulations for worship and also an earthly sanctuary. [2] A tabernacle was set up. In its first room were the lampstand and the table with its consecrated bread; this was called the Holy Place. [3] Behind the second curtain was a room called the Most Holy Place, [4] which had the golden altar of incense and the gold-covered ark of the covenant. This ark contained the gold jar of manna, Aaron's staff that had budded, and the stone tablets of the covenant. [5] Above the ark were the cherubim of the Glory, overshadowing the atonement cover. But we cannot discuss these things in detail now.

9:6 When everything had been arranged like this, the priests entered regularly into the outer room to carry on their ministry. [7] But only the high priest entered the inner room, and that only once a year, and never without blood, which he offered for himself and for the sins the people had committed in ignorance. [8] The Holy Spirit was showing by this that the way into the Most Holy Place had not yet been disclosed as long as the first tabernacle was still functioning. [9] This is an illustration for the present time, indicating that the gifts and sacrifices being offered were not able to clear the conscience of the worshiper. [10] They are only a matter of food and drink and various ceremonial washings—external regulations applying until the time of the new order.

9:11 But when Christ came as high priest of the good things that are now already here, he went through the greater and more perfect tabernacle that is not made with human hands, that is to say, is not a part of this creation. [12] He did not enter by means of the blood of goats and calves; but he entered the Most Holy Place once for all by his own blood, thus obtaining eternal redemption. [13] The blood of goats and bulls and the ashes of a heifer sprinkled on those who are ceremonially unclean sanctify them so that they are outwardly clean. [14] How much more, then, will the blood of Christ, who through the eternal Spirit offered himself unblemished to God, cleanse our consciences from acts that lead to death, so that we may serve the living God!

9:15 For this reason Christ is the mediator of a new covenant, that those who are called may receive the promised eternal inheritance—now that he has died as a ransom to set them free from the sins committed under the first covenant.

9:16 In the case of a will, it is necessary to prove the death of the one who made it, [17] because a will is in force only when somebody has died; it never takes effect while the one who made it is living. [18] This is why even the first covenant was not put into effect without blood. [19] When Moses had proclaimed every command of the law to all the people, he took the blood of calves, together with water, scarlet wool and branches of hyssop, and sprinkled the scroll and all the people. 20 He said, "This is the blood of the covenant, which God has commanded you to keep." 21 In the same way, he sprinkled with the blood both the tabernacle and everything used in its ceremonies. 22 In fact, the law requires that nearly everything be cleansed with blood, and without the shedding of blood there is no forgiveness.

9:23 It was necessary, then, for the copies of the heavenly things to be purified with these sacrifices, but the heavenly things themselves with better sacrifices than these. 24 For Christ did not enter a sanctuary made with human hands that was only a copy of the true one; he entered heaven itself, now to appear for us in God's presence. 25 Nor did he enter heaven to offer himself again and again, the way the high priest enters the Most Holy Place every year with blood that is not his own. 26 Otherwise Christ would have had to suffer many times since the creation of the world. But he has appeared once for all at the culmination of the ages to do away with sin by the sacrifice of himself. 27 Just as people are destined to die once, and after that to face judgment, 28 so Christ was sacrificed once to take away the sins of many; and he will appear a second time, not to bear sin, but to bring salvation to those who are waiting for him.

THE SON AND SACRIFICE

10:1 The law is only a shadow of the good things that are coming—not the realities themselves. For this reason it can never, by the same sacrifices repeated endlessly year after year, make perfect those who draw near to worship. 2 Otherwise, would they not have stopped being offered? For the worshipers would have been cleansed once for all, and would no longer have felt guilty for their sins. [3] But those sacrifices are an annual reminder of sins. [4] It is impossible for the blood of bulls and goats to take away sins.

10:5 Therefore, when Christ came into the world, he said:

> "Sacrifice and offering you did not desire,
>   but a body you prepared for me;
> [6] with burnt offerings and sin offerings
>   you were not pleased.
> [7] Then I said, 'Here I am—it is written
>   about me in the scroll—
> I have come to do your will, my God.'"

10:8 First he said, "Sacrifices and offerings, burnt offerings and sin offerings you did not desire, nor were you pleased with them"—though they were offered in accordance with the law. [9] Then he said, "Here I am, I have come to do your will." He sets aside the first to establish the second. [10] And by that will, we have been made holy through the sacrifice of the body of Jesus Christ once for all.

10:11 Day after day every priest stands and performs his religious duties; again and again he offers the same sacrifices, which can never take away sins. [12] But when this priest had offered for all time one sacrifice for sins, he sat down at the right hand of God, [13] and since that time he waits for his enemies to be made his footstool. [14] For by one sacrifice he has made perfect forever those who are being made holy.

10:15 The Holy Spirit also testifies to us about this. First he says:

> **10:16** "This is the covenant I will make with them
>   after that time, says the Lord.
> I will put my laws in their hearts,
>   and I will write them on their minds."

10:17 Then he adds:

"Their sins and lawless acts
I will remember no more."

10:18 And where these have been forgiven, sacrifice for sin is no longer necessary.

THE SON AND FAITH

11:1 Now faith is confidence in what we hope for and assurance about what we do not see. ² This is what the ancients were commended for.

11:3 By faith we understand that the universe was formed at God's command, so that what is seen was not made out of what was visible.

11:4 By faith Abel brought God a better offering than Cain did. By faith he was commended as righteous, when God spoke well of his offerings. And by faith Abel still speaks, even though he is dead.

11:5 By faith Enoch was taken from this life, so that he did not experience death: "He could not be found, because God had taken him away." For before he was taken, he was commended as one who pleased God. ⁶ And without faith it is impossible to please God, because anyone who comes to him must believe that he exists and that he rewards those who earnestly seek him.

11:7 By faith Noah, when warned about things not yet seen, in holy fear built an ark to save his family. By his faith he condemned the world and became heir of the righteousness that is in keeping with faith.

11:8 By faith Abraham, when called to go to a place he would later receive as his inheritance, obeyed and went, even though he did not know where he was going. [9] By faith he made his home in the promised land like a stranger in a foreign country; he lived in tents, as did Isaac and Jacob, who were heirs with him of the same promise. [10] For he was looking forward to the city with foundations, whose architect and builder is God. [11] And by faith even Sarah, who was past childbearing age, was enabled to bear children because she considered him faithful who had made the promise. [12] And so from this one man, and he as good as dead, came descendants as numerous as the stars in the sky and as countless as the sand on the seashore.

11:13 All these people were still living by faith when they died. They did not receive the things promised; they only saw them and welcomed them from a distance, admitting that they were foreigners and strangers on earth. [14] People who say such things show that they are looking for a country of their own. [15] If they had been thinking of the country they had left, they would have had opportunity to return. [16] Instead, they were longing for a better country—a heavenly one. Therefore God is not ashamed to be called their God, for he has prepared a city for them.

11:17 By faith Abraham, when God tested him, offered Isaac as a sacrifice. He who had embraced the promises was about to sacrifice his one and only son, [18] even though God had said to him, "It is through Isaac that your offspring will be reckoned." [19] Abraham reasoned that God could even raise the dead, and so in a manner of speaking he did receive Isaac back from death.

11:20 By faith Isaac blessed Jacob and Esau in regard to their future.

11:21 By faith Jacob, when he was dying, blessed each of Joseph's sons, and worshiped as he leaned on the top of his staff.

11:22 By faith Joseph, when his end was near, spoke about the exodus of the Israelites from Egypt and gave instructions concerning the burial of his bones.

11:23 By faith Moses' parents hid him for three months after he was born, because they saw he was no ordinary child, and they were not afraid of the king's edict.

11:24 By faith Moses, when he had grown up, refused to be known as the son of Pharaoh's daughter. [25] He chose to be mistreated along with the people of God rather than to enjoy the fleeting pleasures of sin. [26] He regarded disgrace for the sake of Christ as of greater value than the treasures of Egypt, because he was looking ahead to his reward. [27] By faith he left Egypt, not fearing the king's anger; he persevered because he saw him who is invisible. [28] By faith he kept the Passover and the application of blood, so that the destroyer of the firstborn would not touch the firstborn of Israel.

11:29 By faith the people passed through the Red Sea as on dry land; but when the Egyptians tried to do so, they were drowned.

11:30 By faith the walls of Jericho fell, after the army had marched around them for seven days.

11:31 By faith the prostitute Rahab, because she welcomed the spies, was not killed with those who were disobedient.

11:32 And what more shall I say? I do not have time to tell about Gideon, Barak, Samson and Jephthah, about David and Samuel and the prophets, [33] who through faith conquered kingdoms, administered justice, and gained what was promised; who shut the mouths of lions, [34] quenched the fury of the flames, and escaped the edge of the sword; whose weakness was turned to strength; and who became powerful in battle and routed foreign armies. [35] Women received back their dead, raised to life again. There were others who were tortured, refusing to be released so that they might gain an even better resurrection. [36] Some faced jeers and flogging, and even chains and imprisonment. [37] They were put to death by stoning; they were sawed in two; they were killed by the sword. They went about in sheepskins and goatskins, destitute, persecuted and mistreated—[38] the world was not worthy of them. They wandered in deserts and mountains, living in caves and in holes in the ground.

11:39 These were all commended for their faith, yet none of them received what had been promised, [40] since God had planned something better for us so that only together with us would they be made perfect.

12:1 Therefore, since we are surrounded by such a great cloud of witnesses, let us throw off everything that hinders and the sin that so easily entangles. And let us run with perseverance the race marked out for us, [2] fixing our eyes on Jesus, the pioneer and perfecter of faith. For the joy set before him he endured the cross, scorning its shame, and sat down at the right hand of the throne of God. [3] Consider him who endured such opposition from sinners, so that you will not grow weary and lose heart.

CONCLUDING EXHORTATIONS

13:1 Keep on loving one another as brothers and sisters. [2] Do not forget to show hospitality to strangers, for by so doing some people have shown hospitality to angels without knowing it. [3] Continue to remember those in prison as if you were together with them in prison, and those who are mistreated as if you yourselves were suffering.

13:4 Marriage should be honored by all, and the marriage bed kept pure, for God will judge the adulterer and all the sexually immoral.

[5] Keep your lives free from the love of money and be content with what you have, because God has said,

"Never will I leave you;
    never will I forsake you."

13:6 So we say with confidence,

"The Lord is my helper; I will not be afraid.
    What can mere mortals do to me?"

13:7 Remember your leaders, who spoke the word of God to you. Consider the outcome of their way of life and imitate their faith. [8] Jesus Christ is the same yesterday and today and forever.

13:9 Do not be carried away by all kinds of strange teachings. It is good for our hearts to be strengthened by grace, not by eating ceremonial foods, which is of no benefit to those who do so. [10] We have an altar from which those who minister at the tabernacle have no right to eat.

13:11 The high priest carries the blood of animals into the Most Holy Place as a sin offering, but the bodies are burned outside the camp. [12] And so Jesus also suffered outside the city gate to make the people holy through his own blood. [13] Let us, then, go to him outside the camp, bearing the disgrace he bore. [14] For here we do not have an enduring city, but we are looking for the city that is to come.

13:15 Through Jesus, therefore, let us continually offer to God a sacrifice of praise—the fruit of lips that openly profess his name. [16] And do not forget to do good and to share with others, for with such sacrifices God is pleased.

13:17 Have confidence in your leaders and submit to their authority, because they keep watch over you as those who must give an account. Do this so that their work will be a joy, not a burden, for that would be of no benefit to you.

13:18 Pray for us. We are sure that we have a clear conscience and desire to live honorably in every way.

[19] I particularly urge you to pray so that I may be restored to you soon.

BENEDICTION AND
FINAL GREETINGS

13:20 Now may the God of peace, who through the blood of the eternal covenant brought back from the dead our Lord Jesus, that great Shepherd of the sheep, [21] equip you with everything good for doing his will, and may he work in us what is pleasing to him, through Jesus Christ, to whom be glory for ever and ever. Amen.

13:22 Brothers and sisters, I urge you to bear with my word of exhortation, for in fact I have written to you quite briefly.

13:23 I want you to know that our brother Timothy has been released. If he arrives soon, I will come with him to see you.

13:24 Greet all your leaders and all the Lord's people. Those from Italy send you their greetings.

13:25 Grace be with you all.

Also Available in the
New Testament Everyday Series

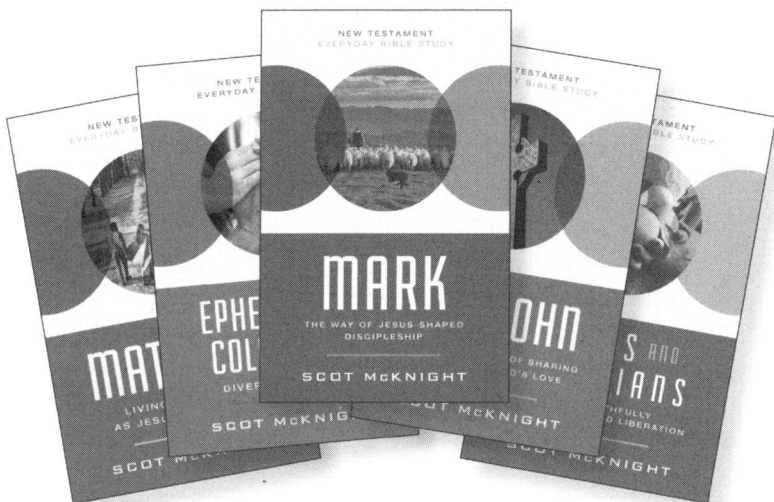